COLOUR FOR MEN

COLOUR

FOR MEN

CAROLE JACKSON
WITH KALIA LULOW

PIATKUS BOOKS

© 1984 Color Me Beautiful Inc.
This edition published by arrangement with
Ballantine Books, a division of Random House Inc.

This edition first published in
Great Britain in 1984 by
Judy Piatkus (Publishers) Ltd
5 Windmill Street, London W1

Reprinted 1988
Reprinted 1990
Reprinted 1992

ISBN 0 86188 365 9
ISBN 0 86188 376 4 (pbk.)

Printed and bound in Great Britain by
Butler & Tanner Ltd, Frome and London

CONTENTS

PART I: YOUR COLOURS

1   COLOUR FOR MEN: WHAT'S IN IT FOR YOU?   9

2   RIGHT/WRONG   11

3   THE SEASONAL PALETTES: THE COLOUR CHARTS   14

4   DETERMINING YOUR SEASON: THE COLOUR TEST   33

5   UNDERSTANDING YOUR COLOURS   48

PART 2: YOUR CLOTHES, YOUR STYLE

6   BUILDING A WARDROBE: CONTENT, COLOUR, LIFESTYLE   71

7   YOUR BODY PROPORTIONS   84

8   YOUR SUIT: SIZE, CUT, FIT AND QUALITY   97

9   YOUR SHIRT   108

10 YOUR TIE **118**

11 CO-ORDINATING JACKET, SHIRT AND TIE **130**

12 YOUR CLOTHING PERSONALITY **139**

13 SHOPPING **159**

14 THE FINISHING TOUCHES: HAIR, GLASSES AND GROOMING **172**

Epilogue: The Total Man **180**

Index **181**

Acknowledgements **183**

PART ONE

YOUR COLOURS

CHAPTER ONE

COLOUR FOR MEN: WHAT'S IN IT FOR YOU?

☐ Do you look your best *all* the time?
☐ Do you project authority and confidence in a business suit?
☐ Can you combine your jacket, shirt, and tie with complete confidence?
☐ Do you have the right thing to wear for any occasion all year round?
☐ Do you have a well co-ordinated wardrobe – or a wardrobe full of unmatched clothes?
☐ Do you hate shopping?
☐ Do you let your girlfriend or wife buy all your clothes?
☐ Do you shy away from peach, pink, or turquoise?
☐ Do you know what colours look best on you?

If even *one* of your answers does not please you, this book is for you. *Colour for Men* is about colour, image and you. It's about using colour to enhance your looks and your life. Yes, colour is the secret of a good image. And what man doesn't want to look his best?

Colour for Men gives a way of dressing in colours that bring out the best in you. Your genes have determined the colour of your skin, your hair and your eyes. Only certain colours complement your natural colouring. When you wear the right colours, you come alive. Dressed in colours that work against what nature has given you, you fade away. I have seen a man change from a frog to a prince simply by changing his shirt!

The key is knowing which colours work best on you. The Colour for Men system will help you discover your personal colours. You will know exactly what clothes to buy – and what not to buy. The system will simplify shopping and help you co-ordinate your wardrobe with ease. Its beauty is that all your colours harmonise so you can mix and match easily. Best of all, dressed in the right colours, you'll look and feel terrific all the time.

We use the seasons as a way of describing your colouring and the colours that look best on you. Nature has done an outstanding job of arranging colours harmoniously, so we borrow from her to create a harmonious wardrobe for you. You are a Winter, a Summer, Autumn or Spring.

The Winter man looks most striking in cool colours with sharp contrast. The Summer man's colouring is most complemented by the cool, dusty colours of summertime. Autumn is the man who looks best in rich warm colours and muted earth tones. The Spring man's colouring is brought to life in the fresh colours of spring.

We are happy to share the power of colour with you. This book will take you through the Colour for Men system. First you'll identify your season, then we'll provide you with a palette of colours that work together. You'll learn how to assemble a well co-ordinated wardrobe with something to wear for every occasion. The Colour for Men system shows you how to co-ordinate a shirt, tie and suit, how to choose accessories, even which hairstyle is most flattering to your face. You'll also find a guide at the end of this book containing a summary of shopping tips for each season.

CHAPTER TWO

RIGHT/WRONG

No matter what season *you* are, some colours work for you and some don't. Wearing the right colour enhances your face. You look younger, healthier, more handsome, more vital and more confident. Facial lines and shadows are smoothed away, your skin glows, your eyes sparkle. You project a positive image to both men and women.

The wrong colour detracts from you. It can make you look tired, sallow or drain the natural colour from your face. Dark circles, lines and blemishes stand out. Wearing the wrong colour may make your clothes overpower your face; people will focus on your clothes instead of on you. Your capability and your authority are undermined because you do not project a harmonious image. In social and romantic settings, you may be turning yourself from a prince into a frog.

Don't panic. The good news is that you can wear almost any colour in the rainbow; the tone, shade, and intensity make the difference. Knowing what colours look good on you lets you make subtle adjustments to your wardrobe that have enormous impact on how the world sees you – and on how you feel about yourself.

You can see from the photographs what a difference colour makes. Your face has colour (skin tone) and your clothes have colour. They react to each other just like colours on a colour wheel. Two colours placed together can bring out the best in each other – or the worst.

You are probably intuitive about your best colours. Look in your own wardrobe. Isn't there a particular shirt you end up wearing every weekend, or a suit in which you feel especially good (even if it is old)? Then there's that almost new item of clothing that you never wear. Why? Most likely it's because of the colour. It looked fine on the rack in the shop, but it just doesn't work on *you*.

COLOUR FOR MEN

Men's intuitive colour sense about what looks good on them is often stifled by their wives or girlfriends, their mothers or salespeople; they all instinctively try to dress other people in *their* colours. Everybody favours his or her own best colours. If you rely on other people who don't know your colours to do your shopping, you'll end up with a wardrobe that is out of step with your natural colour sense *and* that clashes with your natural good looks. (It is also worth noting that 1 in 12 men is colour blind; colour blindness is much rarer in women.)

While Winters and Summers do look their best in the usual business colours, Autumns and Springs, who are flattered by warm, golden colours, must find shades of navy and grey that both project a corporate image *and* work with their colouring. It is hard to look competent with a drawn, tired-looking face, yet many men undermine their image by adopting the 'successful' look without regard for what works for them individually. All men have the freedom to find their own power colours in their own best shades and combinations.

An executive came to us for a consultation. He was wearing a dark grey pinstriped suit, white shirt and burgundy tie. The clothes looked great, but Bill, an Autumn, looked terrible. We showed him how to find his version of grey and how an Autumn uses the right shirt and tie to wear a navy suit effectively. (Navy is not an Autumn's best colour.) We changed his tie from burgundy to a shade of red that flattered him. Result: Bill had an image that was entirely appropriate for his job, but with added *personal* credibility.

David, an overweight middle-aged man, began to feel that life was passing him by. His wife started to tease him about his 'mid-life crisis', until she noticed that he wasn't laughing. To give his self-image a boost, she coaxed him into having his colours done. Sceptical at first, David learned that he is a Spring. A modest sort of man, he wanted to keep wearing 'safe' colours, but he needed to get away from white and dark blue and to experiment instead with some more interesting and more flattering shades.

David bought a new camel-coloured jacket and wore it out to dinner. The response was immediate and dramatic. Had he changed his glasses? Cut his hair? Lost weight? Not yet. But soon, with the confidence he gained from learning his best colours, David found the impetus to do all three.

The effectiveness of personal colours applies to any man, whether he's a doctor, a plumber, an executive, a grandfather or a teenager. Test it yourself! The results are immediate. Buy a couple of casual knitted shirts or T-shirts in colours that bring out your best, and watch the positive response you get from those around you. Try a new tie and shirt in your colours and give your working image a boost. It's important that you get feedback from others, since you'll find it difficult to be objective about your own appearance.

Once you know your colours, you will be able to look good consistently and to believe in yourself all the time. You really *can* colour your way to the top.

CHAPTER THREE

THE SEASONAL PALETTES: THE COLOUR CHARTS

In order to determine your own colours, look at the charts in this chapter. The four seasonal charts are the building blocks of the Colour for Men system. After you understand how the colours work and study the pictures of the men in each season, you can move on to the next chapter to decide which palette is right for you.

UNDERSTANDING THE FOUR SEASONS

The Colour for Men system uses the seasons to describe your colouring and the colour palette that flatters you. Each season conjures an image of colours that everyone understands, and just as in nature, the colours within each seasonal palette harmonise perfectly. The four charts are *not* designed for use during the appropriate season of the year; instead, you belong to one season all year round. By using your season's chart as a guide, you'll be able to match your own colouring to the colours that are best for you, as well as put together a well co-ordinated wardrobe in which your clothes go together effortlessly.

The Winter man looks best in vivid colours, dark colours, or very light, icy shades – say, a navy suit with a pure white shirt and red tie. The Summer man wears pastels and muted dark colours best; a blue shirt and blue suit are his favourites. Autumn is most harmonious in rich, deep earth colours, browns and russets, or muted gold-based shades from medium to dark. And Spring is the man most flattered by warm, golden colours, clear rather than dusty, light to medium rather than dark. A Spring man loves his camel jacket.

COMPARING THE COLOURS

Winter and Summer are the cool (blue-based) palettes. The Winter chart has either blue-based colours or true colours (those with a balance of yellow and blue, black and white). The Summer colours have blue, rose or grey undertones. Autumn and Spring are the warm (yellow-based) palettes. The Autumn palette is based on golden tones, and Spring's colours have clear yellow undertones.

The comparison table at the beginning of the charts shows some of the basic differences among the four seasonal palettes. First look at the different *shades and tones*. Notice how Winter's navy is clear and dark, Summer's navy is greyish, Autumn's is a marine navy and Spring's is a bright, clear royal navy. Now look at the greens. Winter's is a true green, Summer's is a blue green, Autumn's green is golden and earthy, and Spring's is a clear yellow green. The reds for both Winter and Summer are blue reds, because they are the cool (blue-based) seasons; the reds for the warm (yellow-based) Autumn and Spring are orange reds.

Now examine the comparison chart for colour *intensity*. Even though Winter and Summer are both cool, the intensity of their colours differs considerably. Summer's colours may be either clear or powdered (muted), while Winter's are all bold and intense. Compare Summer's light sky blue to Winter's deep royal blue. Autumn has strong colours, either vivid or muted, but Spring has only clear colours. Spring's palette can be bright or light, but never muted or extremely dark. Look at the difference between the browns and yellows of Autumn and Spring.

Now look at the colour charts. Notice that a few colours are missing from some palettes. Only the Winter man can wear both black and pure white, but Winter has no brown or orange. Only Autumn has dark brown, but Autumn has no grey, pink, or purple. Summer has no orange. Spring has a little of every colour except black and snow white.

ANALYSING YOUR COLOURING

Your skin tone, like your palette, is either cool (blue-based) or warm (yellow-based). As we have already said, you can wear almost every colour; the tone, shade, and intensity make the difference. A yellow green, for example, reflects differently on your face than a blue green does; a powder blue has a different effect than a bright blue.

Studying the colouring of the men in the pictures will help you understand why one seasonal chart works best for one individual while another chart works best for someone else. For example, look at the difference between Winter and Summer men. Winter colouring is stronger, with more contrast between hair, skin and eyes. The Summer man has softer, less intense colouring. Even though both are from the cool seasons, a Winter man looks washed out in a pastel sky blue shirt and a Summer's face is overpowered in bright royal blue. In general, notice how much darker the Autumn men's hair and eyes are compared to the lighter colouring of the Springs. Even a light Autumn requires deep, muted colours to enhance his earthy colouring. Bright Spring colours would look brassy on him. Spring, on the other hand, has a clear, lively quality to his skin and eyes, and looks drab in dark or muted colours.

UNDERSTANDING THE CHARTS

Each colour chart is arranged to fit a man's wardrobe. Once you know your season, you can use your chart not only as a guide for buying clothes but also for choosing accessories, decorating your office and even buying your next car! Notice that the charts are divided into Neutral colours, Basic colours, Light colours and Bright/Accent colours to help you organise your wardrobe and shopping.

Neutrals are colours that go with everything. They form the foundation of your wardrobe. Select *overcoats, suits, jackets*, and *trousers* from this group.

Basic colours are a little more colourful than Neutrals, but are still versatile enough to go with many of your other colours, and they add diversity to your wardrobe. Select *jackets* from this group (also from Neutrals) as well as *sweaters, casual outerwear*, and *trousers*. These colours are often found woven into suit fabrics. Your favourite ties will probably come from this category.

Lights are for *business and dress shirts*. Shirt colours are important, since they are worn next to the face. Lights can also be worn in *sweaters* or *summer trousers and suits*. Your shirt may be worn as a solid, or with stripes or checks from any of your colour groups.

Here are some possible combinations for the various seasons.

Winter: White shirt with Bright Burgundy stripe
Summer: Soft White shirt with Blue stripe
Autumn: Oyster White shirt with Rust stripe
Spring: Ivory shirt with Blue stripe

Comparison Table

WINTER	SUMMER	AUTUMN	SPRING
Cool Colours	Cool Colours	Warm Colours	Warm Colours

You can wear almost any colour; the tone, shade, and intensity count. Winter's and Summer's colours are cool with blue undertones. Autumn's and Spring's colours have yellow undertones. One column is best for you.

Winter business/dress

NEUTRAL COLOURS
Suits, Jackets, Trousers

Navy

Charcoal Grey

Black

Medium True Grey

Taupe (Grey Beige)

Light True Grey

LIGHT COLOURS
Business/Dress Shirts

Pure White

Icy Pink

Icy Grey

Icy Green

Icy Blue

Icy Violet

Icy Yellow

Icy Aqua

Ties Colours from any category. Choose from Neutrals or Basics for a conservative look; from any colour for leisure wear.

Shoes and belts (dress) Black, Navy.

Shoes and belts (casual) Black, Navy, Burgundy-toned, Grey. Add Taupe and White for warm weather.

Briefcase and other leather goods Black, Burgundy-toned.

Shopping guide Winters look best in clear colours with high contrast. A Winter strives to stay sharp and should never wear muted, powdered tones. When shopping, think true, blue and vivid; sharp, clear and icy.

Winter leisure wear

BASIC COLOURS
Jackets, Slacks,
Outerwear

BRIGHT/ACCENT COLOURS
Casual Wear

True Blue

Royal Purple

True Red

Lemon Yellow

Pine Green

Fuchsia

Emerald Green

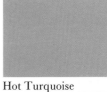

Chinese Blue

Bright Burgundy

Magenta

True Green

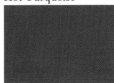

Hot Turquoise

Blue Red

Deep Hot Pink

Light True Green

Royal Blue

Shocking Pink

Summer business/dress

NEUTRAL COLOURS
Suits, Jackets, Trousers

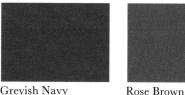
Greyish Navy

Rose Brown

Charcoal Blue Grey

Cocoa

Light Blue Grey

Rose Beige

Greyish Blue

LIGHT COLOURS
Business/Dress Shirts

Soft White

Pale Lemon Yellow

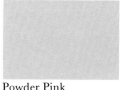
Light Rose Beige

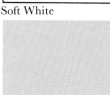
Powder Pink

Powder Blue

Light Mauve

Light Periwinkle Blue

Lavender

Ties Colours from any category. Choose from Neutrals or Basics for a conservative look; any colour for leisure wear.

Shoes and belts (dress) Rose Brown, Black, Burgundy-toned.

Shoes and belts (casual) Rose Brown, Burgundy-toned, Navy, Grey. Add Rose Beige and Soft White for warm weather.

Briefcase and other leather goods Rose Brown, Burgundy-toned.

Shopping guide Summers wear soft Neutrals especially well and may wear both muted and clear colours. When you shop, think of blue or rose undertones. Even though you may favour your bright colours, you should strive for blends and subtle contrasts rather than extremely sharp contrasts. Your dark colours are always greyish.

Summer leisure wear

BASIC COLOURS
Jackets, Slacks,
Outerwear

BRIGHT/ACCENT COLOURS
Casual wear

Cadet Blue

Light Lemon Yellow

Medium Blue Green

Orchid

Burgundy

Sky Blue

Deep Blue Green

Mauve

Blue-Red

Medium Blue

Watermelon Red

Raspberry

Spruce Green

Periwinkle Blue

Pastel Pink

Soft Fuchsia

Pastel Aqua

Rose Pink

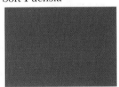

Plum

Pastel Blue Green

Deep Rose

Autumn business/dress

NEUTRAL COLOURS
Suits, Jackets, Trousers

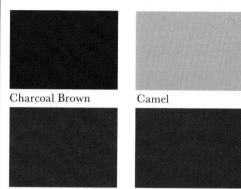

Charcoal Brown

Camel

Dark Chocolate Brown

Marine Navy

Coffee Brown

Olive Green

Khaki/Tan

Greyish Green

LIGHT COLOURS
Business/Dress Shirts

Oyster White

Light Peach/Apricot

Warm Beige

Light Periwinkle Blue

Light Gold

Light Greyish Green

Ties Colours from any category. Choose from Neutrals or Basics for a conservative look; any colour for leisure wear. Reds are acceptable for business as well as for social wear.

Shoes and belts (dress) Brown, Burgundy (brownish); Black (optional – to wear with Navy).

Shoes and belts (casual) Brown, Burgundy (brownish), Tan. Add Beige and Oyster for warm weather.

Briefcase and other leather goods All shades of Brown, Tan, Beige.

Shopping guide Autumns can wear either muted or clear colours. You may use most of these colours as a general guide, but stick closely to the chart when shopping for your blues. Always think of golden undertones.

Autumn leisure wear

BASIC COLOURS
Jackets, Slacks,
Outerwear

BRIGHT/ACCENT COLOURS
Casual wear

Forest Green

Yellow Gold

Orange

Lime Green

Medium Warm Bronze

Mustard

Orange Red

Moss Green

Rust

Pumpkin

Bittersweet Red

Bright Yellow Green

Mahogany

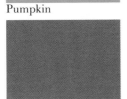

Terra Cotta

Dark Tomato Red

Turquoise

Gold

Deep Peach/Apricot

Jade Green

Deep Periwinkle Blue

Teal Blue

Salmon

Spring business/dress

NEUTRAL COLOURS
Suits, Jackets, Trousers

Clear Bright Navy

Chocolate Brown

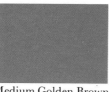
Medium Warm Grey

Medium Golden Brown

Light Warm Grey

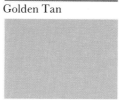
Golden Tan

Light Warm Beige

Camel

LIGHT COLOURS
Business/Dress Shirts

Ivory

Warm Pastel Pink

Buff

Light Clear Blue

Light Peach/Apricot

Light Periwinkle Blue

Ties Colours from any category. Choose from Neutrals or Basics for a conservative look; any colour for leisure wear. Red is acceptable for business as well as for social wear.

Shoes and belts (dress) Brown, Burgundy (brownish), Black (optional – to wear with Navy).

Shoes and belts (casual) Brown, Burgundy (brownish), Tan, Navy. Add Beige and Ivory for warm weather.

Briefcase and other leather goods Brown, Tan, Navy, Beige.

Shopping guide Springs need colours that are 'alive'. When you shop think clear, warm (yellow), and snappy. Your colours are the hardest to find because they must be clear – never muted – and not too dark.

Spring leisure wear

BASIC COLOURS
Jackets, Slacks,
Outerwear

BRIGHT/ACCENT COLOURS
Casual wear

Light Clear Navy

Pastel Yellow Green

Periwinkle Blue

Bright Warm Pink

Light Clear Gold

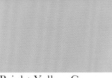

Bright Yellow Green

Dark Periwinkle Blue

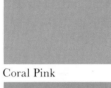

Coral Pink

Light Rust

Light Warm Aqua

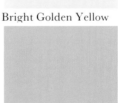

Medium Violet

Bright Coral

Light Teal Blue

Clear Bright Aqua

Bright Golden Yellow

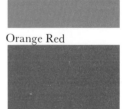

Light Orange

Emerald Turquoise

Peach/Apricot

Orange Red

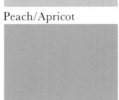

Light True Blue

Clear Salmon

Clear Bright Red

Carl's navy jacket, pure white shirt and striped tie flatter his olive skin and dark hair and eyes.

The light true green and lemon yellow of Ben's sweater and sports shirt complement his rose-beige skin, grey-green eyes and silver-grey hair.

The clear winter colours Martin is wearing set off his black-brown hair, hazel eyes and rosy complexion.

Winter's pure white and royal blue look good with Toshio's olive skin. Olive-skinned Winters look best in clear colours.

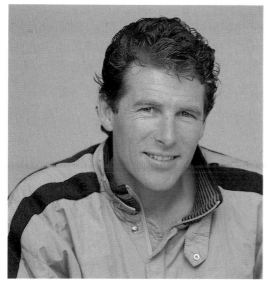

Jack's choice of rose beige as the dominant colour complements his mid-brown hair, clear blue eyes and beige skin.

Terry is a typical Summer, with pink-beige skin and blue eyes. He looks best in the blue and blue-red tonings that flatter his colouring.

Sam's vivid Summer colouring is flattered by his choice of blue, rose-pink and watermelon tonings in his shirt.

Summer's shades of powder blue and blue grey with raspberry-toned tie look good with Bob's clear, light colouring.

Richard's red hair, dark green eyes and ruddy complexion make him a typical Autumn who looks best in clear, definite colours.

Paul's choice of a casual jacket in a terra-cotta and his vividly patterned shirt with green, red and blue tonings flatters his Autumn colouring.

Addison's charcoal black hair and golden brown skin are complemented by his choice of oyster white shirt and shirt and tie in coffee brown tonings.

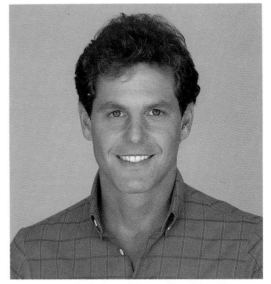

Ken's peach-beige skin and golden brown hair are flattered by his choice of Autumn's bittersweet red and tan tonings.

SPRING MEN

Robert's light periwinkle blue sweater and creamy white shirt complement his hair, eyes and ruddy peach-brown skin tone.

John's strawberry blonde hair, turquoise eyes and light peach skin are emphasised by his colours of clear aqua and buff.

Jim's choice of light clear blue and beige and camel tonings look good with his pale blue eyes, peach-beige skin and warm grey hair.

Barry's jacket in light warm beige and aqua striped tie with ivory white shirt are very flattering to his warm-toned skin and hair.

Bright/accent colours are your chance to add a new dimension to your wardrobe in *casual clothes* and *ties*. Casual clothes may be worn in Brights, as solids or in stripes or other prints, according to your personality.

Although these categories suggest appropriate clothing from each section of the colour chart, the divisions are flexible. For example, Neutral colours, while most suitable for dress or business, may also be worn in casual wear. Ties may come from any category, depending upon your needs and personality.

The seasonal charts are designed to give you a complete range of colours, with something appropriate for every time of year and for every occasion. Some of your colours are suitable for winter, some for summer. Your chart contains business colours, dress colours, casual colours, subdued colours and bright colours.

THE COLOUR FOR MEN SYSTEM

Now you've seen the colour charts and the photographs, you may still feel you can successfully wear colours from all four seasons. Certainly you can find a few from each that may look good on you; some colours are relatively flattering to everyone. But for two reasons you should not wear colours from a palette that is not yours. First, your season's colours are designed to be your *best:* why only look good when you can look great? Second, the colours within each chart are compatible and are arranged to give you a co-ordinated wardrobe. When you follow your chart's guidelines, all your shirts will go with all your trousers. Your ties will go easily with many of your suits and shirts. If you add a colour that does not go with your palette, you throw the whole system out of balance.

To see how the system works, pick out a suit colour from one of the charts. Now imagine each shirt on that chart with the suit. Almost every light colour works. Now choose another suit colour and do the same. Do you see how versatile it is? Each suit can be worn with at least five shirt colours plus all sorts of shirts that include stripes, checks or subtle prints. By adding five or six ties, you can have infinite variety (up to twenty different combinations) from just one suit, especially if it is in a solid colour.

As you build your wardrobe using your own colour chart, you will rapidly experience the true benefits of mix-and-match colours. You'll need fewer clothes, yet you'll have more to wear than ever before. You needn't be frustrated trying to get dressed in the morning, nor will you need to hang shirt and tie on the same coathanger to remember what goes with what; because your colours go with each other, your clothes will co-ordinate all by themselves.

THE SEASONAL PALETTES

Perhaps you are afraid you'll have to give up a colour you really like. If you're unhappy to have to part with a particular jacket, for instance, consider this: did you ever really get a compliment in it? Or did the jacket get the praise? A true compliment is about you, not your clothes, and I promise you that as you wear your new colours and the compliments flow, you'll gladly part with a colour or two. Eventually you will discover that you don't even like that old colour as much as you thought you did: you were probably led astray by fashion or somebody else's taste.

Perhaps you feel limited by the thought of wearing only one set of colours. In reality, however, you will have more options than you've ever had before. Most men are bored by conventional dress codes. Although you may make only subtle changes in your business attire, your leisure clothes will now offer you a wider range of new colours. No need to be afraid of trying them – you know you'll look great!

The biggest bonus in finding your colours is the freedom it brings. Using your chart, you'll spend less time and energy shopping, yet you'll have more confidence than ever before in what you buy and how you look. You'll know what to look for and what to leave on the racks. You'll have a wardrobe of clothes you really like, with something appropriate for any occasion. Your colours will simplify your life, leaving your valuable time free for other pursuits.

Now go on to the exciting part – finding your colours!

Winter/right

Winter/wrong

Carl's darkish, definite colouring is best complemented by the dramatically contrasted colours of Winter. The beige jacket makes his skin look sallow, and lighter colours tend to take colour from his face and eyes.

Spring/right

Spring/wrong

Barry, a Spring, looks good in his beige coat, ivory white shirt and aqua tie. The dark navy jacket tends to drain the colour from his face and the red tie is the wrong-coloured accent. He would look better in a brighter navy jacket and lighter-toned tie.

CHAPTER FOUR

DETERMINING YOUR SEASON: THE COLOUR TEST

To find your season, you'll need to take a three-step test.

1. Assess your colour history.
2. Evaluate your skin tone, hair colour, and eye colour.
3. Test yourself in colours (optional).

You can take this test by yourself or you can ask others to help you. It's hard for us to be objective about ourselves, and other opinions can be helpful.

If you're not a do-it-yourselfer, you may want to skip this chapter entirely and go to a consultant for a personal colour analysis. Once you know your season, you can use the rest of the book to create an image that will truly reflect you.

STEP 1: YOUR COLOUR HISTORY

Here we want to find key colours you feel you have consistently worn with success throughout your life. This test is not based on image, but purely on flattering your face. Image is important, but it comes after you know your season.

Think of your most successful clothes

First, think of compliments you have received. Are people particularly responsive to you when you wear a certain suit or shirt? Don't dwell only on the clothes currently in your wardrobe. They may be right, but they may reflect current fashion rather than being colours that truly flatter.

What colours made you feel good as a child? Your intuition was probably better then because you weren't yet influenced by the dictates of the adult male world. One word of caution: if your mother bought all your clothes and she is a different season, she might have dressed you in her colours all through your child-hood.

Now think of yourself in your favourite weekend clothes. Because of the business dress code, men often pick the Winter or Summer palettes because these seasons contain the most 'businesslike' colours. When a man tells me he thinks he's a Winter but that all his casual weekend clothes are browns and beiges, I can be almost certain that he is an Autumn, simply dressing in greys and blues during the working week and wearing what really suits him on weekends.

Select a column

Now look at the groups of colours below and select the one you feel is most flattering to you. Think of all the colours in the columns as a casual shirt, turtleneck or sweater. Pick the group containing the most colours that have brought you compliments all your life, even if you're tired of wearing them. This test is based on comparison. Each column may have some colours that you have worn, but do they all look equally good on you? Ask yourself, 'Which group is *best*?'

WINTER	SUMMER	AUTUMN	SPRING
Navy	Greyish Navy	Dark Brown	Camel
Black	Blue Grey	Rust	Golden Brown
Charcoal Grey	Sky Blue	Khaki	Light Clear Blue
Burgundy	Rose Brown	Forest Green	Bright Blue
Royal Blue	Burgundy	Olive Green	Turquoise
Red	Pink	Dark Peach	Peach
Pure White	Soft White	Oyster White	Ivory

After you select one column, turn to that season's colour chart in Chapter Three. Does the whole palette seem to suit you?

If you feel pretty confident of your choice, go on to Step 2.

If you're unsure

If you are deciding between two seasons, check out the colour charts for both. Which one is more you? If you're stuck between two seasons, ask yourself the following questions.

DETERMINING YOUR SEASON

If you are deciding between Winter and Autumn, ask
■ Does my face look better when I'm wearing a navy jacket, white shirt and red tie (Winter) or, say, a brown tweedy jacket, beige shirt and rust tie (Autumn)?
■ Do I need strong, clear colours (Winter), or can I wear muted earth tones (Autumn)? Brown-eyed Winters sometimes mistake themselves for Autumns. A Winter looks good only in a very dark black-brown (not on Winter's colour chart). All other browns are boring on a Winter.

If you are deciding between Winter and Summer, ask
■ Does my face look better in a white bright shirt (Winter) or a blue shirt (Summer) with my grey suit?
■ Can I wear dusty pastel colours (Summer) or do these muted colours make me look washed out (Winter)?

If you are deciding between Autumn and Summer, ask
■ Do I look really good in dark peach, rust and brown (Autumn) or am I much better in light blue, blue-toned pinks and burgundy (Summer)?

If you are deciding between Autumn and Spring, ask
■ Do I look great in dark brown and bittersweet red as well as in muted colours such as mustard and khaki green (Autumn) or am I better in clear medium colours such as medium golden brown, clear red, light orange and light clear gold (Spring)? The Spring man will look drab in muted greyish colours, while the Autumn man looks brassy in the clear, brighter colours that so flatter the Spring.

   If neither of these seasons seems to be working, try Summer. Sometimes a camel coat led you to choose Autumn or Spring. Summer also has beiges and browns and a type of earth quality of its own.

If you are deciding between Spring and Summer, ask
■ Does my face look better in camel, golden brown, salmon and bright blue (Spring) or in greyish rose brown, burgundy, blue-toned pinks and medium blue (Summer)?

If you are deciding between Spring and Winter, ask
■ Do I look great in a camel coat (Spring) or do I look much better in a dark navy (Winter)?
■ Am I really good in ivory and golden browns (Spring) or am I better in white

and dark colours (Winter)? A Winter man usually recognises quickly how bad his face looks when he is wearing camel.

STEP 2: EVALUATING YOUR COLOURING

Now examine your colouring to see if it confirms your choice in Step 1.

First, take a good look at your skin tone, hair colour and eye colour. Study yourself in a mirror, preferably in natural daylight. Give yourself a close shave so your facial tone is not influenced by the colour of your beard. A man with a heavy beard will have to look at other parts of his body. If you colour your hair to cover grey or for any other reason, you will need to remember your natural hair colour.

Your skin tone is the most influential factor in determining what colours look best on you. Because the skin is translucent, the tone just under its surface determines whether your colouring is warm or cool. The cool seasons, Winter and Summer, have a blue or greyish undertone to the skin, while the warm Autumns and Springs have a golden or peach undertone.

Some people's skin tone is obvious, but for others the reading can be confusing, and it requires a trained eye. Don't worry if you can't get a clear determination of your skin tone; it is only one part of the test and the other steps will give you enough information to make a decision. Comparison is helpful. Hold a piece of white paper against your palm or your stomach. Is your skin pink or even greyish next to the white, or does it have an ivory or peach cast?

Be careful not to confuse sallowness with a golden skin tone. Many people have sallow skin, which appears yellow on the surface regardless of the undertone. These people are often Winters who will turn even more sallow wearing golden-based colours.

Ruddiness can also be confusing. In a ruddy complexion, the capillaries are very close to the surface of the skin, giving an intense pinkness to the face, especially to the cheeks and nose. This should not be confused with a blue undertone, as, ironically, ruddiness occurs most often in Autumns and Springs, the warm seasons. Here it's best to look at your chest and stomach.

On the following pages are more complete descriptions of skin tone, hair and eyes for each season. Read only the season you selected in Step 1. If it fits, you skip Step 3 and go on with the rest of the book. If it doesn't fit, read the description of your second choice from Step 1.

After weighing your answers to Steps 1 and 2, and looking at the male prototypes in the previous chapter, pick whichever season you feel suits you best.

WINTER

Skin   A Winter's blue undertone is often subtle and difficult to see. There are many varieties of Winter, yet they all need the same cool colours to look their best. Many Winters have grey-beige skin, ranging from light to dark, usually with no visible pink. Most olive-skinned people, blacks and Asians are Winters, though it is possible to find them in any of the seasons.

Many Winters are sallow, appearing yellow, and they wrongly diagnose themselves as Autumns. Wearing golden colours increases the sallowness of their complexion, while the cool Winter colours make the sallowness disappear. A Winter may also have extremely white skin and dark hair. The white may have a visible pink tone, but more often does not. Winters usually do not have rosy cheeks.

Hair   Winters usually have medium to dark brown or black hair, often glossy. The Winter man tends to go grey dramatically, either reaching a salt-and-pepper stage or turning steely white. Hair that goes grey prematurely is a sign of Winter or Summer. Winter hair usually has an ash tone, although sometimes the hair will have red highlights visible in sunlight (this is not the metallic red seen in Autumn hair, however). Occasionally a Winter has white-blonde hair as a child, but has turned dark by the age of five or six and is quite dark in adulthood. It is rare to see a blonde Winter adult, but when it happens, his hair is often very blonde and he is indeed a striking man.

Eyes   Winter eyes can be black-brown, red brown, green, blue or hazel, and are most often a deep colour. The green or blue eyes of a Winter are distinguished by white flecks in the iris and often a grey rim around the edge of the iris. The hazel-eyed Winter usually has a brown smudge with jagged edges surrounding the pupil, with either blue or green extending to the outer iris. Occasionally a green-eyed Winter has a single thick yellow line going from the pupil to the edge of the iris like a single spoke on a wheel.

In general, all Winter eyes tend to have a look of high contrast between the whites of the eyes and the iris. This clue is especially helpful if you are deciding between Winter and Summer, as the white of a Summer eye is usually much softer with less contrast in the iris.

Winter prototypes
Burt Reynolds, Omar Sharif, Dustin Hoffman, Christopher Reeve, Imran Khan, Clive Lloyd, Alan Bates

COLOUR FOR MEN

Tick the characteristics that describe you.

Skin
- ☐ Very white
- ☐ White with slight pink tone
- ☐ Beige (no cheek colour, may be sallow)
- ☐ Grey beige or brown
- ☐ Rosy beige
- ☐ Olive
- ☐ Black (blue undertone)
- ☐ Black (sallow)

Hair
- ☐ Blue black
- ☐ Dark brown (may have red highlights)
- ☐ Medium ash brown
- ☐ Salt and pepper
- ☐ Silver grey
- ☐ White blonde (rare)
- ☐ White

Eyes
- ☐ Dark red brown
- ☐ Black-brown
- ☐ Hazel (brown plus blue or green)
- ☐ Grey blue
- ☐ Blue with white flecks in iris (may have grey rim)
- ☐ Dark blue, violet
- ☐ Grey green
- ☐ Green with white flecks in iris (may have grey rim)

SUMMER

Skin Summers often have visible pink in their skin, so it is easy to see the blue undertone. Some Summers are very fair and pale and have little pink rings under the skin on the whitest parts of their bodies. The skin may have a translucent quality. Other Summers have rose-beige skin or sallow beige skin, making the blue undertone difficult to see. A sallow Summer makes an especially dramatic improvement in his appearance when he wears his cool colours.

Hair   As a child, Summer is often blonde, his hair colour ranging from white to ash blonde. During adolescence his hair tends to darken, and by secondary school age it has usually turned a light ash (greyish) brown. Summer blondes bleach quickly in the sun, so often a Summer man has brown hair in the winter and blonde hair in summer. If he spends lots of time outdoors, his blonde hair may become golden, which can make him look deceptively like a Spring. (To judge your hair colour accurately, look at the roots. If they are not golden, you are probably a Summer.) Brunette Summers also have hair with an ash tone, ranging from light to dark brown. Usually a very dark-haired Summer has extremely light skin, and visible pink in his cheeks. Occasionally a Summer has auburn hair (slightly red brown) and can be confused with an Autumn. A Summer usually tans, while an Autumn more often burns. The Summer man's hair greys pleasantly to soft salt and pepper, blue grey or pearly white. Grey is a cool colour that blends well with the ash tones of his hair, giving him a distinguished look. One caution: On a Summer man, a beard or sideburns often grow in red. Use only the hair on top of your head to do this analysis.

Eyes   Summer eyes are usually blue, green, grey or hazel, with a cloudy look to the iris. Often there is a grey rim around the edge of the iris, or the entire eye colour looks greyish. Hazel eyes have a soft, grey-brown smudge around the pupil with edges blending into blue or green. The iris in a blue or green eye has a white webbing throughout, giving the appearance of cracked glass. Some Summers have soft rose brown or grey-brown eyes. The whites of a Summer's eyes are creamy, in soft contrast to the iris, as opposed to a Winter, whose eyes have sharp contrast.

Summer prototypes
Paul Newman, Christopher Atkins, Jimmy Stewart, Alan Alda

Tick the characteristics that describe you.

Skin
☐ Pale beige with pink cheeks
☐ Beige with no cheek colour (even sallow)
☐ Rosy beige
☐ Very pink

☐ Grey brown
☐ Rosy brown

Hair
☐ White blonde
☐ Ash blonde
☐ Warm ash blonde (slightly golden)
☐ Dark ash blonde
☐ Ash brown
☐ Dark brown (taupe tone)
☐ Brown with auburn cast
☐ Blue grey
☐ Pearl white

Eyes
☐ Blue (with white webbing in iris, cloudy look)
☐ Green (with white webbing in iris, cloudy look)
☐ Soft grey-blue
☐ Soft grey-green
☐ Bright, clear blue
☐ Pale, clear aqua (eyes change from blue to green, depending on clothes)
☐ Hazel (cloudy brown smudge with blue or green)
☐ Pale grey
☐ Soft rose brown
☐ Grey-brown

AUTUMN

Skin Look for the golden undertone. Autumns come in three varieties: the fair-skinned man with ivory or creamy peach skin; the true redhead, often with freckles, and the golden beige man whose skin ranges from medium to deep copper. Many Autumns are pale and will look better in their darker or richer colours. Autumn men often burn in the sun and cannot get a tan. Autumns and Springs often have similar colouring, but the Autumn man usually has no cheek colour, and the Spring does. On the other hand, some Autumns are ruddy and may look pink, but the pink is more peachy than blue. These Autumns look good in a few

Summer colours, but really come to life in the true Autumn palette. A few Asians and blacks are Autumns if their skin has a truly golden undertone, but most are other seasons.

Hair   Autumn's hair is usually touched with red or golden highlights. It ranges from auburn to copper, strawberry blonde to red, dark golden blonde to warm brown. Some blonde Autumns have hair often referred to as 'dirty blonde', and these men can easily be confused with Summers. A few swarthy Autumns have charcoal black hair. Autumn hair, except for that of a few auburns and dark brunettes, tends to have a matt rather than a shiny finish. The Autumn man usually does not go grey dramatically because the grey may detract from his warm-toned hair. Once his hair has turned completely grey, it looks harmonious and has a warm, golden cast. During the in-between stage, he may prefer to colour the grey with a warm tone as close to his original as possible.

Eyes   Autumn eyes are usually golden brown or green with orange or golden streaks radiating from a star formation that surrounds the pupil. Sometimes there are isolated brown specks in the iris. Some Autumns have clear green eyes, like glass, or deep olive green cat eyes. There are a few vivid blue (turquoise) and steel blue Autumn eyes that are marked by a teal grey rim around the edge of the iris. Occasionally an Autumn man has extremely pale blue or teal blue eyes, giving the appearance of a clear ring around the pupil. He is a pastel Autumn, looking best in the muted colours of the palette.

Autumn prototypes
Robert Redford, Charlton Heston, Woody Allen, Michael Jackson, Michael Yorke

Tick the characteristics that describe you.

Skin
- ☐ Ivory
- ☐ Ivory with freckles (usually redhead)
- ☐ Peach
- ☐ Peach with freckles (usually golden blonde, brown)
- ☐ Golden beige
- ☐ Dark beige (coppery)
- ☐ Golden brown

Hair
- ☐ Red
- ☐ Coppery brown
- ☐ Auburn
- ☐ Golden brown (dark honey)
- ☐ Golden blonde (honey)
- ☐ 'Dirty' blonde
- ☐ Strawberry blonde
- ☐ Charcoal brown or black
- ☐ Golden grey
- ☐ Oyster white

Eyes
- ☐ Dark brown
- ☐ Golden brown
- ☐ Amber
- ☐ Hazel (golden brown, green, gold)
- ☐ Green (with brown or gold flecks)
- ☐ Clear green
- ☐ Olive green
- ☐ Steel blue
- ☐ Teal blue
- ☐ Bright turquoise

SPRING

Skin Look for the golden undertone. The Spring man's skin is ivory, peachy pink or golden beige, and he often has rosy cheeks or blushes easily. Some Springs are ruddy and can easily be confused with Summers because of their apparent pinkness. Even their knuckles may look purple. (If this describes you, look at the parts of your body that aren't ruddy to see the true tone.) Freckles, usually a golden tan colour, come naturally to the Spring man. Other Springs have clear, creamy skin. Even if he has freckles, the Spring man's skin usually has a clear, bright quality. Black and Asian Springs have light, golden skin.

Hair Spring's hair is flaxen blonde, yellow blonde, honey, strawberry or golden brown. Spring doesn't have ash-tone hair, as Summer does. In childhood many

DETERMINING YOUR SEASON

Springs are blonde, but their hair usually darkens with age. An occasional Spring has dark brown hair. Grey usually arrives in a yellow or cream tone on a Spring. If his hair is light, the grey often blends beautifully, making him look 'blonde'. On a dark-haired Spring, the grey may detract from the golden tone of his hair. The Spring man may want to cover his grey until his hair has gone completely grey. Once the two-tone look is gone, his grey hair is beautiful, with a pale, warm, dove-grey tone. Spring men often go from grey to a creamy white, a softly elegant look for them.

Eyes   Spring's eyes are most often blue, green, teal or aqua, often with golden flecks in the iris. Some Spring men have eyes as clear as glass, giving the impression of a clear ring surrounding the pupil. Most Spring eyes have a 'sunburst' around the pupil. Inside the sunburst you may see a 'doughnut' tightly surrounding the pupil. Fibres radiate from the edge of the sunburst to the edge of the iris, much like the spokes of a wheel. Some Springs have brown eyes, but they are always golden or topaz. A Spring's hazel eyes contain golden brown, green and gold. A few Spring men have eyes of deep blue that appear to be steel grey from a distance.

Spring prototypes
Michael Caine, David Bowie

Tick the characteristics that describe you.

Skin
- ☐ Creamy ivory
- ☐ Ivory with golden freckles
- ☐ Peach
- ☐ Peach/pink (may have pink/purple knuckles)
- ☐ Golden beige
- ☐ Golden brown
- ☐ Rosy cheeks (may blush easily)

Hair
- ☐ Flaxen blonde
- ☐ Yellow blonde
- ☐ Honey blonde

☐ Strawberry blonde (usually with freckles)
☐ Strawberry redhead (usually with freckles)
☐ Auburn
☐ Golden brown
☐ Red black (rare)
☐ Dove grey
☐ Creamy white

Eyes
☐ Blue with white rays
☐ Clear blue
☐ Steel blue
☐ Green with golden flecks
☐ Clear green
☐ Aqua
☐ Teal
☐ Golden brown

By now you should know your correct season. Do not be too technical about analysing yourself: *what looks good on you* is the best test of all.

If you want to verify your choice or if you are still trying to decide between two seasons, take Step 3 and see yourself in the colours. Otherwise go on to **Chapter 5** to learn how to use your colours.

STEP 3: SEEING YOURSELF IN TEST COLOURS

Some people are genetically on the cusp of two seasons, and holding the colours under your face will help you see which season is *best*. You may look pretty good in some colours from one season, but on the whole look better in another palette. Never judge by one colour alone.

This test is based on comparision. You should compare one colour against another, perhaps several times, to see which is better.

In the box following, locate the two seasons you are trying to decide between.

To make the decision:

■ Gather the colours of the two seasons in question. Any solid-colour fabric will do (shirts, towels, scarves, a child's T-shirt).

DETERMINING YOUR SEASON

■ Give yourself a close shave so you can really see your skin tone.
■ Find a place with bright natural daylight or bring a mirror to a window. Fluorescent light changes the colour of both your skin tone and the fabric colours.
■ Ask for some outside opinions. People tend to favour their own colours, so ask more than one person in order to avoid individual bias.
■ Hold the colours under your face, using the combinations suggested above. Place the two test colours on top of each other and hold them under your face. Look at the effect of the top colour for a few seconds, then peel it off so you can see the effect of the second colour. Repeat several times. Then go onto the next two colours. Remember, this test is based on comparison. One colour may look all right, but the other will be better.

AUTUMN	or	WINTER	SUMMER	or	SPRING
Brown	or	Navy	Burgundy	or	Light Orange
Warm Beige	or	Pure White	Rose Brown	or	Golden Brown
Rust	or	Blue Red	Blue Pink	or	Peach/Apricot
AUTUMN	or	**SPRING**	**SUMMER**	or	**WINTER**
Dark Chocolate Brown	or	Medium Golden Brown	Rose Brown	or	Black
Mustard	or	Light Clear Gold	Soft White	or	Pure White
Khaki	or	Ivory	Medium Blue	or	Royal Blue
AUTUMN	or	**SUMMER**	**WINTER**	or	**SPRING**
Rust	or	Blue Red	Black	or	Camel
Moss Green	or	Blue Green	Pure White	or	Ivory
Teal Blue	or	Powder Blue	Burgundy	or	Light Orange

There are two rules.

1. **Be objective.** Try not to be influenced by your favourite and least favourite colours.
2. **Look at your face, not at the colour.**

Here's what to look for as you compare the colours under your face.

Right Colour

The colour smooths and clarifies your face. It minimises the beard line, shadows and circles under the eyes. It makes wrinkles or lines at the side of the mouth and nose blend smoothly into your face. It brings out a healthy glow in your skin. It makes your eyes sparkle. Your face stands out, pushing the colour into the background. The colour harmonises with your face.

Wrong Colour

The colour may make your face look pale, sallow or 'dirty'. It will accentuate a heavy beard, lines, wrinkles or shadows under the eyes. It will accentuate any blotches or scars. It dulls your eyes. It may age your face, especially if you are over thirty. The colour will look too strong or too weak, in either case making your face fade into the background. The colour does not harmonise with your face.

Here are the questions most frequently asked.

Can I be more than one season?
Not really. Some men are on the cusp of two seasons, but with testing, one palette will prove to be better than the other. Even if more than one colour chart appeals to you, you are doing yourself a disservice to mix the palettes. Each chart is designed to create an automatically co-ordinated wardrobe, so 'borrowing' from different palettes defeats the system. Remember, your genes determine your skin tone, hair colour and eye colour, which in turn determine the colours that look best on you. Your best colours are not a matter of taste, but of fact.

Does my season change with a tan?
No. Your genetically determined skin tone doesn't change; it simply darkens with a tan or fades somewhat with age. The same seasonal palette will always be best for you.

When you are tanned you can wear 'wrong' colours more successfully, but why do it? You'll ruin your image and your wardrobe.

Does my season change when my hair gets grey?
No. However, once your hair is grey you may prefer to wear the lighter or softer

colours from *your* palette. Your most flattering neutral colours will be those that harmonise with your hair – your season's greys and blues.

Now that you've assessed your colour history, evaluated your colouring and possibly even tested yourself in colours, you should feel confident that you know your correct season. Now begins the pleasure of wearing your colours. Try out your season by wearing something you already own in your colours. The compliments you receive will confirm your choice.

CHAPTER FIVE

UNDERSTANDING YOUR COLOURS

Your seasonal colour chart makes it easy to look good. But beyond co-ordinating your wardrobe, your colours also define your image and express your personality. Once you understand the colours themselves and have a *concept* of your season, you will be able to determine which colours within your palette are best for *you*, as well as to shop easily for your colours when you buy clothes. This chapter will focus on individualising your colours, on using your colours in business and leisure wear and on understanding the colours themselves when you shop.

INDIVIDUALISING YOUR COLOURS

By now you may be thinking, 'I'm a Winter with pale skin and John's a Winter, too, but with dark olive skin. How can we both use the same colour chart as a guide?'

Each season does encompass a wide range of people with different intensities of colouring, but your season's colour chart may be interpreted to suit you as an individual. Most men wear all their colours well, but some, depending upon their hair colour and the depth of their skin tone, wear some colours better than others close to the face. If you are fair, some of the brightest colours may overpower your face and are best reserved for use as an accent in a tie or a striped shirt. By the same token, if you look best in the stronger shades from your season, mix your paler colours and neutrals with other, more intense colours. Use the pale colours as accents in prints and away from the face. *All* your colours are valuable to you because they give you infinite variety and the ability to build a co-ordinated and flattering wardrobe.

UNDERSTANDING YOUR COLOURS

Your personality also influences how you will use your seasonal colours. Some men are comfortable only in conservative colours, even in leisure wear, while others are more daring. Suit yourself. Each colour chart has conservative as well as bold colours. All the colours will flatter you, but you will be most successful when you interpret your palette to reflect your personality.

Your image is another consideration. Whatever your season, you can project the image you desire. Each chart provides you with the opportunity to be authoritative or low-key, sophisticated or casual, formal or informal. While one Autumn may prefer to dress with high contrast and project an image of power, another Autumn may want an elegant but understated monochromatic look.

Finally, each season can be interpreted so it reflects *your mood*. There are colours in your palette to express any mood, on a daily basis or even in yearly trends. You may spend several years in the mood for bright colours and then swing to a desire for calm ones.

USING YOUR BUSINESS COLOURS

In many professions, men want an image that conveys power and authority on some days and the co-operative team player on others. Many men work in offices and shops that require a degree of conformity to a standard dress code. A well-groomed, conservative image is the most effective. If you happen to work in a profession or business that allows more individual style – journalism, for example, or advertising – you can afford to be less conservative.

Businessmen have traditionally dressed in navy, grey and black, but not all men can wear the standard business colours with equal success. You need to adapt the image appropriate for your profession to your season so that you can both look good *and* project your desired image.

Keep in mind the following general rules to make your business dressing effective and attractive.

■ When your goal is to convey authority, wear your season's dark colours. Navy is the favourite, but Autumns may want to consider charcoal brown.
■ Wear your season's greys and/or browns or rust when you want a lower-key image. A jacket, if your profession allows it, is always less serious or authoritative than a suit.

■ Create the strongest *overall* image for you by wearing the right colours for *you*. You can make subtle adjustments to your business wardrobe without having to break the dress code of your work environment. Be sure to wear the right colours in your shirt and tie. You'll look better and consequently others will see you more favourably.

USING YOUR COLOURS IN CASUAL CLOTHES

The world of casual dressing ranges from sporty to sharp, high fashion to casual, rugged to sensual. Here is your chance to explore your colours and your character freely. The bright colours on each chart offer a bounty of special sporty colours. By using them as accents or in combination with more subdued neutrals and light colours, you can find new ways of expressing your style.

The safest way to wear your bright colours is to buy your trousers in neutral, conservative colours and try the bright or unusual colours in shirts. If you have an outgoing, unconventional personality, you can go all the way with colourful trousers and jackets. You will still look good as long as you stick to your palette because the colours will go together and will go with you. The only time you'll call negative attention to yourself is if you wear a daring colour that is wrong for you.

If you want to try a colour but are unsure that you will feel comfortable wearing it, buy it in an inexpensive T-shirt. When you get compliments, you will start liking that colour.

The Seasonal Palettes

Following is a basic explanation of each season's colours. Because it is difficult to print the colour swatches 100 per cent accurately, these verbal descriptions will help you understand the concept of your colours when you shop for clothes. In addition, I've added specific information for each season on individualising your colours – as well as how to use them in business clothes and casual wear. Read only your season, then skip to the end of this chapter, where you will find a chart comparing your colours with those of the other seasons.

WINTER

Winter colours are intense. Your Winter image depends on sharp contrast and clear colours. A clear colour looks pure and 'clean'. Never wear anything dull or muted, especially in ties. Look for the sharp navies and reds rather than the muted ones. In general you wear dark colours, vivid colours, or very light, icy colours – no pastels for you.

Here is the Winter palette.

■ White

Winter is the only season with pure white. A Winter man is never boring in a white shirt! You can also wear Summer's soft white (but *not* ivory or yellowish white), thought it will not be quite as dashing on you as the bright white.

■ Black

Winter is also the only season who can wear black. You look great in dark colours, and any of your colours may get darker and darker until they look almost black.

■ Grey

Your greys range from charcoal to icy grey. They must be true greys, not yellowish or blue. Once your hair has turned completely grey, you may add blue greys to your palette.

■ Taupe (Grey Beige)

Your beige is *not* tan-toned, but grey beige (taupe). When worn near the face, it must be light and clear. You may choose a darker shade in trousers, shoes, and leather goods. Beige in general is a difficult colour for a Winter to wear.

■ Blue

Navy blue is excellent on you. You may wear any shade of navy near the face except grey navy. Your other blues are true, royal, Chinese and turquoise, all deep or bright.

■ Red

Winter's reds are either true or blue reds, including burgundy. Your burgundy must be clear, sharp and bright, rather than a muted or brownish tone.

■ Green

Your greens range from a true green to emerald to pine. Pine is similar to Autumn's forest green except that it has a blue cast rather than a yellow tone. You can see this difference by comparing the two colours side by side. Winter men who previously never liked green often discover that they love *their* greens.

■ Yellow

Your yellow is special. You can wear only a clear lemon yellow that does not verge on gold at all. Stick closely to your yellow when shopping; it's hard to find.

■ Pink and Purple

Winter's pinks and purples are deep colours. The shocking and deep hot pinks are less conservative, while magenta and fuchsia are quite sophisticated colours.

■ Icy Colours

Icy colours are unique to the Winter palette. You can wear any of your colours in an icy version, including taupe and grey. An icy colour is clear and sharp, like wearing white with a hint of colour added. Your icy colours are blue, violet, pink, green, yellow and aqua. Be careful not to buy a Summer's pastel shirt instead of your icy tone. You will lose the sharp contrast that brightens your face and makes your Winter image so effective.

Avoid all colours with golden undertones, such as orange, rust, peach, gold, yellow green, orange red, tans and browns. If you must wear brown, choose a black brown that is dark enough to wear with black shoes and belt. Avoid pastels and all dusty, muted colours. When shopping you may use your chart as a general guideline for all colours except your yellow and taupe (grey beige), which should be matched as closely as possible.

Individualising Your Colours

The fair-skinned Winter man may find that soft white is better than pure white, and may also find that the icy and the darkest colours are better for him than the true, bright colours. Dark-skinned Winters may find that taupe and the light and medium greys are best when worn mixed with other, brighter colours near the face. Some Asians and olive-skinned men who are very sallow will not wear burgundy, fuchsias or their pinks as effectively as their other colours. A Winter with sandy brown or grey hair may add powder blue to his palette; although it is a Summer colour, a lighter-haired Winter can wear it.

Business Colours

Winters have the easiest time shopping for standard business clothes. Black, navy and grey suits all look good on you. You may have trouble in the summer, however, finding your version of a tan suit. Every now and again your taupe appears as a fashion colour. Don't compromise; the usual beige or light brown suits look absolutely wrong on a Winter.

Your best business suit is white, but the icy colours in your chart give you extra leeway for conservative yet stylish dressing. Icy pink and violet are suitable for some business environments and are excellent for evening dress. Icy green is usually best with a sports jacket. Aqua is best with a dinner jacket or in a sporty cotton shirt. You will usually find your icy colours in designer shirts. The usual blue business shirts are best for Summers. If you can't find icy blue, choose the lightest clear blue you can find.

Your best ties come from your red family. Any dark blue red or brightly burgundy tie, solid or patterned, is an excellent business look for you, as is a dark navy tie, especially if it has some red or white accents in it.

A taupe trenchcoat is hard to find, as most of the beige trenchcoats are not your tone. If you cannot find your grey beige, consider navy or grey.

Leisure Wear Colours

You can't beat a Winter in a navy blazer. This will make you feel better when you pass by the camel jackets, leaving them on the rack for the Springs or Autumns. Tweeds, even in your colours, usually look less good on you than solids. A pair of grey or navy trousers will go with everything in your palette.

SUMMER

The Summer palette gains its strength from a harmonious blend of tones, even in its most vivid shades. The Summer man's image is enhanced by soft contrasts and subtle colour combinations. His dark colours should be slightly grey or greyish in order to avoid looking harsh or overpowering his natural colouring. He can wear either clear or muted colours in his pastel and medium shades.

The Summer palette is as follows.

■ Soft White
The Summer man's most flattering white is a soft (but not yellow) one. It is less 'blue' than Winter's pure white.

■ Rose Beige and Brown
Your beige must always have a rose cast, rather than an ivory or yellow tone. You can wear browns from medium to darkish as long as they, too, are rose-toned. Your browns are especially flattering if they are muted (greyish).

■ Blue Grey
Summer may wear all blue greys from light to dark, but should avoid true greys or yellowish greys. Greys devoid of blue will look dead on a Summer.

COLOUR FOR MEN

■ Blue
Your navy is a greyish navy, more flattering to you than a bright or black navy. You may wear almost all other blues, light, medium, or dark, but not the extremely bright or royal blues of Winter. Your blues may be clear or muted, and your lighter blue suits will have lots of grey in them. When using aqua-toned blues, keep them soft. You can also wear periwinkle, a blue with violet in it.

■ Green
Your greens are all in the blue green family, ranging from a light pastel shirt colour to medium blue green colours to a dark spruce green. Your spruce green, like your navy, is a little greyer than Winter's. This spruce green is especially good on brown-eyed Summers.

■ Yellow
Summer's yellow is a light lemon hue, ranging from pastel to a *slightly* brighter shade. Avoid yellows that are golden.

■ Pink
Your pinks are blue-toned, ranging from light shirt colours to medium shades to deeper rose and fuchsia colours. Although you may wear bright pinks, be careful not to buy the intensely clear and bright shades from the Winter chart.

■ Red
Summer's reds range from raspberry to watermelon to blue reds. You may wear dark blue red as well as burgundy and all wine colours. Unlike Winter, your reds may be either clear and bright or slightly muted.

■ Plum
Plum is your version of purple. It is a greyish purple, not as intense or as dark as the royal purple of Winter. Lavender, orchid and mauve are wonderful colours for you, and they are easily found in both light shades for dress shirts and slightly darker shades for sportswear. You don't have to be careful when selecting these.

Avoid pure white, camel, yellowish beiges, tans and browns, gold, orange, peach, orange reds, yellow greens, and black. Use your chart as a general guideline except when shopping for rose beige and yellow, when you should match the colour as closely as possible.

Individualising Your Colours
Fair Summers with blonde or light hair should keep the darkest colours of burgundy, spruce green and dark blue red as accents, or use them in combination

with a mellowing shirt and tie. Large areas of these dark colours may be too strong right next to your face. Summers with dark brown hair are particularly handsome in the dark colours and in the more vivid colours from the Summer chart. This type of Summer just missed being a Winter. Brown-eyed and green-eyed Summers often look especially good in their browns and greens and should keep their blues and greys mixed with other colours for maximum impact. These Summers are close kin to Autumns, having an earthy quality yet needing cool, blue-based colours to flatter, rather than yellow-based ones.

Business Colours

The Summer palette, like that of Winter, lends itself beautifully to the traditional business colours. Although it is best to find a greyish navy suit when possible, almost any navy that is not too blue and bright will do well for you when combined with your best shirt and tie colours. Besides navy, you have a wide range of suits in lighter blue shades. The medium brown suits that are very acceptable in business are great for you – as long as they have a rose tone. Occasionally you will find a summer suit in rose beige (your tan) but most often the coloured suits will be for Autumns. Don't compromise. The wrong tan will make you look really washed out. You do not wear black, but you can use your dark charcoal suit to serve as black. Because of your relatively lighter colouring, this grey will look dark and authoritative on you. Both your soft white and your charcoal blue grey will appear as strong within your colour chart as black and white do within the Winter chart. The impact of colour is relative within the season and works proportionately with your colouring to create a powerful image. Be sure when buying a grey suit that it is a blue grey. It is easy to spot them hanging on the racks compared to the true and charcoal greys.

Your business shirts are easy to find. Most ready-made pastel shirts are for you. All the blues as well as yellow and rose beige look good for business, in addition to your soft white. In some business situations you can wear your pink or lavender shirts as well. You may even wear a light blue grey shirt, especially if your hair is grey.

For ties, choose your burgundy and blue red, either solids or patterns. Make sure these reds are slightly toned down. Use watermelon red, which is brighter, as a background colour in a tie. Your greyish navy and all shades of blue, mixed with white, grey, silver, mauve or yellow, are great business ties for you.

Your trenchcoat, like your summer suit, may be hard to find in rose beige. If you cannot find one, consider navy.

Leisure Wear Colours

A navy blazer is a great look for you, especially with a blue shirt. For variety you may want to try a spruce green or burgundy blazer in winter or a medium blue, periwinkle or other pastel shade in a summerweight blazer. Many Summers, because of their softer colouring, look great in soft tweeds or even checks in blue and grey, or brown and blue combinations. A pair of blue grey trousers will go with almost everything in your palette. If you favour your browns, buy a pair of cocoa-coloured slacks for maximum versatility.

AUTUMN

Autumn colours can be either clear or muted, but they always have warm golden undertones. A clear colour looks pure and clean; a muted colour is toned down by the addition of brown, grey or gold. Most Autumns prefer their medium or bright colours slightly muted. The Autumn chart gains its power from an artful combination of blended tones with the more assertive, dark colours.

Here are Autumn's best colours.

■ Oyster White

Your best white is oyster (beigeish white). You may also wear ivory (a yellowish white) and the soft white from the Summer palette, but *never* pure white. It will make you look pale.

■ Brown, Beige and Grey

All your beiges and browns are warm earth tones. Your dark chocolate brown and mahogany are rich colours. Camels, khakis, and tans are also good for you. Your bronze is an unusual colour, flattering only to an Autumn. You will need to use dark charcoal brown as your black or charcoal grey and coffee brown as your grey. Coffee is any brown that has grey added.

■ Blue

A marine navy is the only navy that truly flatters the Autumn man but it is hard to find. You can wear any kind of teal blue, though the darker and richer the colour, the better. Your turquoise is medium to dark and has warm yellow undertones. By comparing turquoises in the shop, you can see that some are clear and bright (not for you), while others are yellower and slightly muted – again full-bodied colours. Periwinkle is a blue with a violet cast. In general, you look best in a deep periwinkle.

The Winter's man wardrobe can be subtle, formal or colourful, according to his personality. Charcoal grey, navy and black can be teamed with vivid or more conservative colours to create a varied and interesting combination of shades for all occasions.

Summer's cool colours in shirts, ties, belts and trousers provide an exciting wardrobe of casual to dressy sportswear. Shirts, ties, belts and trousers can combine in a great number and variety of ways for an elegant look.

The rich tones of browns, rusts and jewel colours harmonise to create a varied and colourful wardrobe for Autumn. All clothes have warm undertones to flatter Autumn's colouring, in everything from formal business wear to casual clothes and accessories.

No need to stick to the 'safe' colours for the Spring man! The varied shades of blue, as well as ivory, buff, beige and warmly glowing reds all complement his colouring. The Spring palette provides many fresh, vibrant colours to team in casual and business wear.

UNDERSTANDING YOUR COLOURS

■ Green

Your greens range from dark forest green to olive, jade and greyish greens. You can wear any green that has a golden tone, from subtle to bright. A light, greyish green is excellent.

■ Gold and Yellow

Your golden colours are plentiful. Choose gold in a quality fabric, or the garment you are wearing will look 'cheap and nasty'. You can wear any shade of gold, from mustard to a bright yellow gold.

■ Orange

Your oranges include terracotta and rust colours, which are easy to find in all types of clothing. Your pumpkin and bright orange are leisure colours, good in prints or in solids for the less conservative.

■ Peach and Salmon

Your best peach, apricot, and salmon shades are deep. Use the light versions mixed with darker or brighter colours to add oomph. Salmon is your version of pink.

■ Red

You may wear any red with an orange base, ranging from bright orange-red to bittersweet red and dark tomato (more muted shades). Your reds may get brownish, resembling maroon. Avoid burgundy, as it is too 'blue' and harsh for you, thus bringing out any lines in your face.

Avoid pure white, black and grey. Avoid all pinks, burgundies, blue reds or colours with blue undertones. Keep your pastel colours, as well as peach, salmon, and periwinkle, a medium to dark shade when worn alone near the face (i.e., without the benefit of suit and tie). You may use your chart as a general guideline except when shopping for navy and periwinkle, when you should try to match the colour as closely as possible.

Individualising Your Colours

Autumns can be divided into three categories: the true Autumn, who wears all the colours equally well, the muted Autumn (usually light-haired), who wears the more subtle and muted colours best, and the strong Autumn (usually dark-haired or brightly redheaded), who wears the dark and vivid colours best. A fair Autumn with light hair can be overwhelmed by some of the bright, clear colours such as orange and orange red, so the fair Autumn man should reserve these for use in stripes or prints. This is the Autumn man who just missed being a Spring, but who needs more muted colours than those in the Spring chart. Most dark-skinned Autumns wear the more vivid colours better than beige, khaki, olive, or greyish greens.

Business Colours

Autumn colours do not fit the businessman mould. If you work in a business where the usual navies and greys are standard, you will have to shop more carefully. *Marine navy* is hard to find, though you may be able to find it through a tailor and have a suit tailor-made. If you must compromise on your navy, remember to keep your tie and shirt in your season.

You have a large selection of browns. *Medium browns* are highly acceptable for business wear and come in beautiful fabrics, especially in subtle patterns. For a larger selection than off the racks, go to your favourite men's wear shop and look at the swatches in the books used for selecting tailor-made suits. Your palette does not have grey; use *greyish browns* to achieve the same look. A *charcoal brown* suit has a very similar look to a charcoal grey, and is especially powerful when coupled with a dark red tie from your palette. Subtle business *tweeds* look especially good on you, and they favour your colours – *browns* and *greens*. A little grey mixed in won't hurt, as long as the overall effect is yours. (How do you tell? If it blends with your shirt and tie, it's yours.)

Business shirt colours are also harder for the Autumn man to find. Try to find *oyster white*. You can also wear Summer's soft white or Spring's ivory, but oyster will be your best. (I know one Autumn who dipped his white shirt in weak tea. It worked!) Your *beige, buff,* and *light periwinkle* are good business colours, and in some work environments you can wear *peach* and *greyish green*. When you are shopping for a periwinkle blue dress shirt, be careful not to buy powder blue by accident. Periwinkle has more violet in it and is much more flattering; powder blue will make your face look pale. You can easily see the difference when you shop, as powder blue will clash with periwinkle.

Reds and *navies* are the favourite business ties. Be sure you select your *warm reds* and not the blue-toned reds or burgundies. A dark, muted *bittersweet red* or *brownish red* is your best. A brighter red is acceptable if it is used as a background for a print. Use *navy* only as an accent, as it is hard to find your Autumn shade. Experiment with *browns, periwinkles, rust* and even your darker *greens*. All are acceptable for business.

A trenchcoat for you is no problem to find, as most traditional coats are in your *browns*.

Leisure Wear Colours

In country, elegant or casual clothes, Autumn has the easiest shopping of all the seasons. Your colours are readily available and the Autumn palette lends itself beautifully to sporty attire. In fact, the *tans* and *khakis* look good *only* on Autumns, so you can console yourself when you are searching harder to buy business clothes. You look great in a *rich brown* tweed jacket with texture, and if you are blonde or honey-haired, you will shine in a *camel* jacket. Camel is not as good as a darker colour on the brunette Autumns. Wear lots of leather and leather trim in any of your browns. A pair of *brown* or *rust* trousers will go with everything in your palette.

SPRING

The Spring palette is warm and energetic. The Spring man's colours are friendly and extroverted, as are most Spring personalities. You do not wear dark or heavy colours well, so strive for medium-dark to light shades. All your colours must be clear, which means they look pure and clean. Avoid muted (greyish) colours, as you will look washed out in them.

Here are Spring's colours.

■ Ivory (White)

The Spring man's best white is ivory, a creamy white. He may also wear Summer's soft white, but not Winter's pure white, which will make him look pale.

■ Grey

Your greys must be clear and warm, with yellow undertones, and have a bright, crisp quality. Even in winter you should avoid dark greys. Light greys are your very best. A medium grey will look darkish on you because of your light colouring.

■ Blue

Your most flattering navy is a light, bright one. The next best is a darker but still bright and clear navy. Your other blues range from a light true blue to periwinkle blues, i.e., blues with a violet tone. Your aquas and turquoises are plentiful, ranging from medium to bright. A light clear blue is good on a Spring man. Avoid any blue that is too pale or powdered. You look best in blues with depth or brightness.

■ Brown and Beige

Your beiges and browns range from ivory to clear warm beige to golden tan, camel, medium golden brown, and chocolate brown. You do not wear dark browns or greyish coffee browns. Be sure to avoid wearing any muted or muddy browns, such as khaki, near your face. You can wear khaki trousers.

■ Gold and Yellow
Your gold is light and clear. Buff and chamois colours are wonderful for you, as is bright golden yellow.

■ Red
The Spring man's reds are either orange reds or clear reds. Darker reds are harsh and ageing to your face, so they should be avoided. Spring may also wear light rust.

■ Green
Yellow-greens are for you, ranging from pastel to bright.

■ Pink and Peach
All shades of peach, apricot, coral, salmon and warm pink are for you. You do not have to be careful at all when choosing clothing in this colour family. You wear them from light shades to medium and bright ones. Warm pinks have yellow in them, easy to see when compared to blue pink.

■ Orange
Your orange is fairly light; never as bright as Autumn's orange.

■ Violet
Medium violet is your version of purple. Avoid darker purples; they will look too harsh with a Spring man's colouring.

Individualising Your Colours
Most Springs have good colour in their cheeks and therefore wear all their colours well. If you are a very fair, blonde Spring, you will find that your brightest yellow and yellow green are too strong if large areas of either are worn. If you are a dark-haired Spring, you may find that your camel and palest colours look best when mixed with a more vivid colour.

Business Colours
Spring has the hardest time assembling a business wardrobe because the Spring man's colouring demands medium to light colours and is easily overpowered by dark ones. Try to find the brightest, liveliest navy you can. Avoid greyish navies. Your best grey is a light warm grey, usually found in summer. Medium warm grey is as dark as you should go. Bear in mind that, because of your lighter colouring, a medium grey will look dark on you. Colour is relative. (If you must compromise on either your navy or your grey suit, be sure to wear a shirt and tie from your season.) Spring can wear blue suits in lighter shades than navy, as long as the suit

looks alive rather than drab. You rarely find a medium golden brown wool suit fabric, but you will find chocolate brown as well as tweeds with golden tones. Again in business suits you may have to compromise and verge a bit into Autumn's browns – keeping your shirt and tie in your colours, of course.

Like Autumn, you may need to have your business suits tailor-made to take advantage of the wider selection of fabrics. In summer you will find that some of the beige and golden brown suits are clear and warm – just right for you. A *camel* summer suit is great, if you can find it in a business style.

Business shirts are easy for you to find. Your *ivory light warm beige, buff* and *light periwinkle blues* are excellent for business wear. In addition, you may wear Summer's soft white (but not Winter's pure white – you'll look pale). Your *peach, apricot* and *warm pink* shirts are acceptable in some work environments and they're great as dress shirts for social wear.

Choose a red tie as often as you can. Because your *orange red* is so bright, it will be more suitable for business when used as a background for a print. Your *light clear navy* is great too, as is a *light blue* or *dark periwinkle*. Shades of golden tan, camel, or buff are fine for business, as is light rust or even teal.

A trenchcoat for you is a bit hard to find because many of the beiges are darkish and muted. Choose a beige that is light and clear if possible. Also consider a brightish navy.

Leisure Wear Colours

You're the man who looks really good in a camel jacket. Your golden browns also appear frequently in sports jackets, both as solids and in tweeds. Casual shirts for you offer a wide selection in stripes and plaids, and Spring colours abound in bright shirts. Most Springs enjoy their bright colours. A pair of trousers in beige or golden brown will go with everything in your palette. A special bonus for Spring is your perpetually youthful look – more than compensation for the fact that you have to work harder to assemble a business wardrobe.

Colour Comparison Chart

	WINTER	SUMMER	AUTUMN	SPRING
White	Pure White	Soft White	Oyster White	Ivory
Beige	Taupe *(Grey Beige)*	Rose Beiges *(Light to Medium)*	Warm Beiges Gold Toned Beiges *(including Camel)*	Light Warm Beige Creamy Beiges, *(including Camel)*
Grey	True Greys *(Icy to Charcoal)*	Blue Greys *(Light to Charcoal)*	——	Warm (Yellow) Greys *(Light to Medium)*
Brown	—— ——	Rose Browns Cocoa	*Most Browns:* Charcoal Chocolate, Coffee, Mahogany *Most Tans:* Khaki/Tan, Medium Warm Bronze	Chocolate Brown Medium Golden Browns Golden Tans
Black	Black	No Black	No Black	No Black
Navy	Any Navy	Greyish Navy	Marine Navy	Light Clear Navy Clear Bright Navy

	WINTER	SUMMER	AUTUMN	SPRING
Blue	True Blue Royal Blue Icy Blue	Greyish Blue *(including Denim)* Sky Blue Periwinkle *(Light to Medium)* Cadet Blue Powder to Medium Blue	Teal Periwinkle Blues *(Light to Deep)*	Light Teal Periwinkle Blues *(Light to Dark)* Light Blue Light True Blue
Turquoise	Hot Turquoise Chinese Blue Icy Aqua	Pastel Aqua	Turquoise	Emerald Turquoise Clear Aquas *(Light to Bright)*
Purple	Royal Purple Icy Violet	Plum Soft Fuchsia Mauve *(Light to Medium)* Orchid Lavender	—	Medium Violet
Green	Light True Green True Green Emerald Green Icy Green Pine Green	Blue Greens *(Pastel to Deep)* Spruce Green	Greyish Greens *(Light to Dark)* Yellow Greens *(Light to Bright)* Forest Green Jade Green	Clear Yellow Greens *(Pastel to Bright)*

	WINTER	SUMMER	AUTUMN	SPRING
Orange	—	—	All Oranges Rust Terracotta Peach/Apricot	Light Oranges Salmon Peach/Apricot Bright Coral Light Rust
Pink	Shocking Pink Deep Hot Pink Magenta Fuchsia Icy Pink	Pastel Pinks Rose Pinks *(Medium to Deep)* Powder Pink	Salmon	Warm Pastel Pink Coral Pink Clear Bright Warm Pink Clear Salmon
Red	True Red Blue Reds	Watermelon Red Blue Reds Raspberry	Orange Reds Bittersweet Red Dark Tomato Red	Orange Reds Clear Bright Red
Burgundy	Bright Burgundy	Burgundy *(including Maroons and Brownish Burgundy)*	—	—
Gold	—	—	Golds *(Light Beige-toned to Medium)* Mustard	Light Clear Gold Buff
Yellow	Lemon Yellow Icy Yellow	Pale Lemon Yellow Light Lemon Yellow	Yellow Gold	Bright Golden Yellow

PART TWO

YOUR CLOTHES, YOUR STYLE

CHAPTER SIX

BUILDING A WARDROBE: CONTENT, COLOUR, LIFESTYLE

It's time to put your colours to work and give yourself the pleasure of a wardrobe that works for you.

In order to build a wardrobe, you need to start with a foundation. I call this the Survival Wardrobe. The Survival Wardrobe is the clothing that every man needs to go anywhere and feel and look good. It is simple, well co-ordinated, easy to shop for and foolproof! When you combine your colours with an organised, modular approach, you have assembling a wardrobe down to a science. Whether you are starting to build your wardrobe, correcting your current one or making a change in lifestyle, the Survival Wardrobe makes sure you'll never be caught without something appropriate to wear.

THE SURVIVAL WARDROBE

Getting Started

The effectiveness of your Survival Wardrobe (and the rest of your wardrobe, once you get beyond the basics) is magnified when every single item is from your own colour palette. Because you probably have some wrong colours in your wardrobe to start with, you will not be completely co-ordinated overnight. But if you buy *only* your own colours from now on, you will gradually produce the miracle of an automatically co-ordinated wardrobe.

Phasing out wrong colours can take a few years (those expensive suits!), depending on what you currently own and how much you have to spend. In the meantime, make your wrong-colour suits and trousers work by combining them with shirts and ties from your palette. Get rid of your unflattering shirts and ties, however, if your budget possibly allows. The colours closest to your face count the most.

You may find that there are certain items on the Survival List that you don't need. Fine. Cross them off. One word of caution, however. Think twice before crossing a suit off your list. It can take days, if not weeks, to buy a properly fitting suit. Some students say they have absolutely no use for a suit, but I know of at least one young man who had to attend a good friend's impromptu wedding wearing his father's ill-fitting, wrong-colour, stodgy old suit. He felt miserable. The secret of the Survival Wardrobe is owning it *before* you need it.

Obviously you will need more than one of certain items, depending on your lifestyle. We'll talk about quantity at the end of the chapter. Now the object is to identify the gaps in your wardrobe.

The Survival List

The Survival List includes all the items you need to have a wardrobe that can take you anywhere. On the following pages, the items are described in detail. After you read the descriptions, use the list as a shopping guide. Cross off each item you already have in your colour. This way you can easily see what you *don't* have. If you have an item that's perfectly wearable but not in the right colour, put brackets around it to indicate you'll eventually phase it out; for now it will have to do.

■ Suit

Your survival suit should be a solid-colour neutral in a wool or wool blend fabric. The cut should be conservative and the suit should fit you to perfection. For maximum versatility, choose a dark neutral so the suit will be dressy enough for a wedding but also appropriate for business or less formal social events. For summer, you may choose a lighter colour and certainly a lighter weight fabric.

■ Jacket/Blazer

Choose your most flattering neutral in a solid colour. Use wool blends, corduroy, or ultrasuede for winter and cotton blends or linen-look fabrics for summer. It's fine to buy a tweed or small check instead of a solid if you feel it's more you, but a patterned jacket will be less versatile with your shirts and ties.

■ Slacks

These are your dressy slacks. Buy a solid-colour darkish neutral in a wool or wool blend for winter, and a light to medium shade in a cotton-polyester blend for summer. These trousers must go with your jacket and should be either lighter or darker in order to make a good contrast. Winters and Summers will probably buy greys; Autumns and Springs tans and browns. Choose a plain style. These slacks can go to work or a party when worn with a jacket, or to a sporting event with a checked shirt and sweater.

■ Shirt 1
This is your basic daytime shirt which should be in your season's white. (It's worth the extra effort for Autumns and Springs to search for their harder-to-find shades of white. It really makes a difference!) Choose cotton or cotton-polyester with a button-down or plain collar. Button-downs are more casual. Summers and Springs could substitute a light blue shirt in this category.

■ Shirt 2
For dressier situations, buy a fine cotton, plain-collared shirt in white or a subtle colour from your palette. If the shirt is coloured, make sure it goes with both the suit and the jacket.

■ Shirt 3
Your third shirt is more casual and can be worn with your suit, your jacket and your slacks. Choose either a solid colour or a subtle check or stripe. If your jacket is patterned, you will have to make sure the pattern in this shirt is compatible, or stick to a solid-coloured shirt.

■ Tie 1
Choose a solid tie in a deep basic colour to go with the suit, the jacket and all three shirts. If you have bought a patterned Shirt 3 containing several colours, make sure the solid tie picks up one of the colours in the shirt. When possible, you should pick out the tie first and then the patterned shirt to go with it.

■ Tie 2
This tie is patterned with a small repeat pattern, a stripe or a paisley, depending upon your personality. The background of this tie should be the red of your season or one of your deeper or brighter basic colours, with the pattern picking up the colour of your suit, your shirt or both.

■ Tie 3
Your third tie should be striped. Most men can wear some form of stripe, bold or subtle, depending upon personality. Some portion of this tie must pick up the colour of your suit and, ideally, the colour of your shirt as well. If stripes are too severe for you, then buy one more tie from the Tie 2 category.

■ Belt
Select a leather belt in a dark neutral that harmonises with your season. Winters and Summers should find a silver-toned buckle, as silver is a cool colour that looks

sharper with your palette. Autumns and Springs should choose a gold-toned buckle to harmonise best with your palettes.

■ Business/Dress Shoes

Depending on your personality, buy either leather lace-ups or dressy pull-ons. Choose a neutral colour, preferably the same as your belt. These shoes should go with your suit and slacks above.Don't forget to buy mid-calf or knee-length dark socks so skin doesn't show when you're sitting down with your legs crossed.

■ Casual Slacks

These slacks are casual but not grubby. They can be corduroys, cotton-polyester blends or even a nice pair of jeans, depending upon your lifestyle. You can wear your jeans or corduroys with your jacket if you are a casual sort of man. It's still best to buy your first pair of casual slacks in a neutral colour.

■ Casual Shirt

For winter choose a flannel shirt in a solid colour or with checks, a long-sleeved cotton knit shirt or whatever suits your fancy. For summer, a short-sleeved T-shirt will do fine. Now you can have more fun with the colours. Because you can wear Shirts 1 and 3 with your casual trousers, you can afford to be less conservative with this casual shirt. Most people need to have more than one casual shirt, whatever their lifestyles.

■ Sweater

Choose a favourite neutral or basic colour to go with your nice slacks, your casual slacks and all your shirts. The sweater can be a crewneck, V neck, or rollneck. In summer, a cotton knit or lightweight wool is always useful.

■ Shorts

These shorts are not for active sports but rather for comfortable, presentable wear in hot weather. They can be short, mid-thigh, or just above the knee, depending upon your personality, your age and your legs. Buy any neutral or basic colour or your season's white. A solid is best, but a small check is fine as long as it goes with the short-sleeved cotton knit casual shirt. If the shorts are a solid colour you can wear them with Shirt 3 and partly roll the sleeves up.

■ Casual Belt

Your casual belt may be leather, but it's fine here to have a fabric belt, either plain or striped. If you decide on leather, choose a wider belt.

■ Casual Shoes

Any casual lace-ups will do here, depending on your comfort, age and lifestyle. Tennis shoes and boots fall into this category.

BUILDING A WARDROBE

■ Around the House

Everyone needs 'old' clothes to wear at weekends, to paint the garage in or whatever, and most people already have plenty of these. The point is to keep only those items that are in your colours. You may be spending 90 per cent of your casual time in these clothes, so why look awful at home? T-shirts are inexpensive, so treat yourself to a new one and ditch *all* your bad ones.

■ Coat

Ideally you would buy a wool or cashmere coat in the dressiest neutral colour in your palette. This coat can also be worn for business. The lifestyle of most people has become increasingly casual during the past decade, so you may find that you can skip this purchase. A coat is a major investment, so if you do buy one, choose one in a classic style with no faddish details. You want this coat to last.

■ Trenchcoat

The trench-type coat is probably necessary for every man. It is a perfect business coat and raincoat, and it functions well enough in the evening, except on really formal occasions. Colour? Either the brown or the navy of your season.

■ Jacket

Choose a parka or sheepskin for cold weather; an anorak or any light weight jacket for warmer weather. Choose any colour from your palette. A neutral or basic colour will go with all your clothes, but a brighter colour may add some zip to your life.

■ Cold Weather

If you have cold winters, you will need gloves, a scarf and possibly a pull-on woollen cap. Buy the gloves and cap in neutrals to go with the coat or jacket you wear most often. The scarf can be solid, check or plaid in any colour from your palette.

■ Sports/Hobbies

If you have a hobby or sport – such as tennis, jogging, skiing, or swimming – that requires special attire, don't forget to add these to your own personal survival list. Since shopping is so painful for some, you might as well pick up these needed items while shopping for everything else.

■ Personal

Obviously a man needs underwear for survival, but I am assuming that these personal items – plus pyjamas, dressing-gown and slippers – are already part of your wardrobe, and are replaced from time to time out of sheer necessity.

Finishing Touches

■ Dinner Suit

I have not included a dinner suit in the Survival List because most men rent one on the rare occasion it is needed.

■ Accessories

To complete your wardrobe you will need certain accessories. Be sure your leather goods, pocket handkerchief and other accessories are in colours from your palette. Why spoil the harmony of your total look with one off-key item?

■ Jewellery

Try to have your watch, rings, cuff links and any other jewellery or metals in the hue best for your season. As with your belt buckle, choose silver or silver-toned metals for Winter and Summer and gold or gold-toned metals for Autumn and Spring. If you are a Winter or Summer and feel you must wear gold, choose a toner that is subdued and not too yellow. A bright yellow gold will clash with everything you wear.

The Survival List

Tick off each item in the Survival List you already have in your colour. Then shop to fill in the blanks.

	Cold Weather	Warm Weather
Suit		
Jacket/Blazer		
Shirt 1 (basic daytime)		
Shirt 2 (more dressy)		
Shirt 3 (more casual)		
Tie 1 (solid)		
Tie 2 (patterned)		
Tie 3 (striped)		
Belt		
Business/Dress Shoes		

BUILDING A WARDROBE

	Cold Weather	Warm Weather
Casual Slacks		
Casual Shirt		
Sweater		
Shorts		
Casual Belt		
Casual Shoes		
Around the House		
Coat		
Trenchcoat		
Jacket		
Sports/Hobbies		

On the following pages you will find suggested colours for the major purchases on the Survival List. These are merely suggestions, showing how well everything goes together. Notice that all the shirts go with all the ties, and all shirts and ties go with the suits, jacket and slacks. Don't try to expand your wardrobe by mixing your jacket with the trousers from your suit. This is not a good way to stretch your budget, as the trousers in suits are usually cut differently from slacks and are made from different fabrics, even if the colours are compatible.

The Survival Wardrobe consists mainly of neutral and basic colours. In addition, you will buy most of these items in solid colours. It may seem boring at first, but I assure you this approach will give you the most variety from the fewest items of clothing. As you expand your wardrobe to suit your lifestyle, you can add more colours and patterns to your wardrobe.

Winter Colours

	Cold Weather	Warm Weather
Suit	Charcoal grey	Navy
Jacket/Blazer	Navy	Navy
Slacks	Charcoal grey	Taupe
Shirt 1 *(basic daytime)*	Pure white (cotton or cotton-polyester)	White
Shirt 2 *(more dressy)*	Pure white (cotton or cotton-polyester)	Icy Pink
Shirt 3 *(more casual)*	White with blue stripe	White with grey stripe
Tie 1 *(solid)*	Blue red	Bright burgundy
Tie 2 *(patterned)*	Navy with small white dots	Navy with pink and grey motif
Tie 3 *(striped)*	Bright burgundy, navy and white	Grey with navy, white and blue red
Belt	Black	Black
Business/Dress Shoes	Black	Black
Casual Slacks	Navy	Taupe
Casual Shirt	Burgundy, navy, grey small checks or plaids	Emerald green
Sweater	Burgundy	Lemon yellow
Casual Belt	Navy (fabric)	Dark taupe (fabric)
Casual Shoes	Brownish burgundy	Brownish burgundy
Coat	Navy	——
Trenchcoat	Grey	Grey
Jacket	Navy	True blue

Summer Colours

	Cold Weather	Warm Weather
Suit	Charcoal grey	Greyish navy
Jacket/Blazer	Greyish navy	Medium blue (linen)
Slacks	Charcoal grey	Navy
Shirt 1 (basic daytime)	Blue (cotton or cotton-polyester)	Soft white
Shirt 2 (more dressy)	Soft white (cotton or cotton-polyester)	Soft white
Shirt 3 (more casual)	Sky blue and white stripe	Soft white with grey, navy, or burgundy stripe
Tie 1 (solid)	Burgundy	Deep rose
Tie 2 (patterned)	Watermelon red with sky blue and grey motif	Navy with grey and white motif
Tie 3 (striped)	Rose and light blue-grey	Mauve with navy and white
Belt	Black or brownish burgundy	Black or brownish burgundy
Business/Dress Shoes	Black or brownish burgundy	Black or brownish burgundy
Casual Slacks	Greyish blue	Rose beige
Casual Shirt	Rose pink	Medium blue green
Sweater	Burgundy	Light lemon yellow
Casual Belt	Navy (fabric)	Beige (fabric)
Casual Shoes	Brownish burgundy	Brownish burgundy or Rose brown
Topcoat	Charcoal blue grey	——
Trenchcoat	Greyish navy	Greyish navy
Jacket	Light blue grey	Greyish blue

Autumn Colours

	Cold Weather	Warm Weather
Suit	Charcoal brown	Olive
Jacket/Blazer	Camel	Light tan
Slacks	Dark chocolate brown	Coffee
Shirt 1 *(basic daytime)*	Warm beige	Buff
Shirt 2 *(more dressy)*	Oyster white	Oyster white
Shirt 3 *(more casual)*	Peach/apricot	Light greyish green
Tie 1 *(solid)*	Rust	Bittersweet red
Tie 2 *(patterned)*	Rust, camel, and oyster paisley	Olive with tan and red motif
Tie 3 *(striped)*	Brown with rust and oyster stripes	Brown, camel and olive
Belt	Brown	Brown
Business/Dress Shoes	Brown	Brown
Casual Slacks	Coffee	Khaki
Casual Shirt	Teal blue	Salmon
Sweater	Warm beige	Oyster
Casual Belt	Tan *(fabric)*	Tan *(fabric)*
Casual Shoes	Brownish burgundy	Tan
Coat	Camel	——
Trenchcoat	Khaki	Khaki
Jacket	Mahogany	Coffee

Spring Colours

	Cold Weather	Warm Weather
Suit	Bright navy	Light warm beige
Jacket/Blazer	Camel	Light clear navy
Slacks	Medium golden brown	Light tan/camel
Shirt 1 *(basic daytime)*	Ivory	Light periwinkle blue
Shirt 2 *(more dressy)*	Ivory	Ivory
Shirt 3 *(more casual)*	Soft white with light rust stripe	Warm pastel pink
Tie 1 *(solid)*	Light rust	Navy *(must blend with jacket or blazer)*
Tie 2 *(patterned)*	Orange red with navy and ivory motif	Clear bright red with beige and periwinkle motif
Tie 3 *(striped)*	Navy, rust, ivory and camel	Navy, clear red, ivory, tan
Belt	Brownish burgundy	Brownish burgundy
Business/Dress Shoes	Brownish burgundy	Brownish burgundy
Casual Slacks	Light clear navy	Light warm beige
Casual Shirt	Light clear gold	Peach
Sweater	Apricot	Light periwinkle blue
Casual Belt	Navy *(fabric)*	Tan *(fabric)*
Casual Shoes	Brown	Tan
Coat	Camel	——
Trenchcoat	Light warm beige	Light warm beige
Jacket	Medium golden brown	Light true blue

YOUR LIFESTYLE AND HOW TO DRESS FOR IT

After you have the essentials, you will need to expand certain categories according to your lifestyle. The Survival Wardrobe applies to any man, but your own situation determines what you need to be comfortably outfitted beyond survival.

For the sake of determining quantity, I've identified four lifestyles.

- The City Businessman: Suit every day
- The Professional Man: Suit or jacket every day
- The Casual Man
- The Man in Uniform

See what quantity of each item you need to keep your life running smoothly, and write the numbers on your Survival List, which then becomes your ideal shopping guide.

The City Businessman

You are the man whose job requires you to wear a suit to work every day. You'll need six suits (at least two solids), twelve shirts, and ten ties, plus one or two jackets and one or two pairs of slacks for social wear. The suit-every-day man often has a big gap in his wardrobe – plenty of suits, a pair of jeans, but nothing in between. Buy two pairs of nice casual slacks and at least four casual shirts. And don't forget some casual shoes to augment your lace-ups and your sneakers. You're used to being dressed up all the time, so pay special attention to completing your casual wardrobe.

The Professional Man

Your job allows you the flexibility of wearing either a suit or a jacket to work. Buy three suits (two solids), three jackets, three pairs of slacks, twelve shirts and ten ties. Like the businessman, you need at least two pairs of casual slacks, four casual shirts, and a pair of casual shoes for weekends or evenings that require more than a pair of jeans.

The Casual Man

You may be retired or you may have a job that calls for casual clothes every day. Buy six pairs of casual slacks (at least three should be washable), twelve casual shirts, and two pairs of casual shoes. If your job or daily life allows for jeans and T-shirts, include them in the casual wear suggested. Since you're wearing these every day, be sure they are 'new' and clean. There's a big difference between clean, pressed jeans and tatty jeans and T-shirts with holes in them. To complete your wardrobe, add one suit (solid colour) for dressier occasions, two jackets and two pairs of slacks for social wear, and six shirts and six to ten ties for both.

The Man in Uniform

You may be in the army, navy or air force or you may work somewhere that requires a uniform. Whatever the case, your work clothes are taken care of. You need one solid-colour suit for dressy occasions and one or two jackets and pairs of slacks for social events. In addition to your jeans, T-shirts, and other clothes for wearing around the house, add two casual pairs of slacks, four casual shirts, and a pair of nice casual shoes to complete your non-work wardrobe. If you 'retire' from your uniformed job, you will need to re-evaluate your quantities according to your new lifestyle. It's easy. Just pick another category and follow the guidelines for it.

Now that you know what you really need, you'll be surprised at how easy it is to shop. Remember, shopping ahead of need is the secret to a successful wardrobe – and an organised life! Whatever your lifestyle, with a plan and your colour palette, you can now fill the gaps in your wardrobe and have clothes that really work for you.

CHAPTER SEVEN

YOUR BODY PROPORTIONS

Before shopping for a suit, jacket, slacks or a shirt, you need to be aware of the overall proportions of your body. Are your arms short? Are you high-waisted? Are your shoulders and hips in proportion? Once you understand your body, you can make cut, style and fit work for you to disguise your flaws and create a balanced look.

Since few of us are perfectly proportioned, our goal is to create the *illusion* of perfection. Basic to the illusion is a key principle of design: the eye rests where a line stops. By modifying the lines of your clothes, you can, for example, visually lengthen short legs, diminish a prominent bottom or widen narrow shoulders. A good tailor can make your clothes fit, but only you – by choosing your apparel intelligently – can make line, style, and cut work to your best advantage.

DETERMINING YOUR PROPORTIONS

Stand in front of a full-length mirror so you can examine your overall body harmony. Look at yourself objectively. You may wish to have a tape measure handy and a friend to help you.

The following body checklist shows you the key areas of your body that affect your overall look. After you have read the short explanations that follow, measure and study yourself, then fill in the chart.

■ Height/weight

Everyone has a different personal ideal concerning height and weight. In general, 173 cm (5 ft 8 in) and under is short, 175 cm to 180 cm (5 ft 9 in to 5 ft 11 in) is average, and 182 cm (6 ft) and over is tall. In many cases, actual height and weight are

Body Checklist

Height ☐ tall ☐ average ☐ short

Weight ☐ heavy ☐ average ☐ thin

Shoulder/hip proportion ☐ shoulders much wider than hips
☐ good proportion
☐ hips even with or wider than shoulders

Slope of shoulders ☐ tapered ☐ average ☐ square

One shoulder higher ☐ yes ☐ no

Leg length from hip to floor ☐ long legs
☐ short legs
☐ average proportion

Waist ☐ high ☐ low ☐ average proportion

Neck ☐ long ☐ short ☐ average proportion

Arms ☐ long ☐ short ☐ average proportion

One arm longer ☐ yes ☐ no

Upper back ☐ straight ☐ round

Bottom ☐ prominent ☐ flat ☐ average

less important than the relationship of the body parts to the whole. However, if you want to appear taller, shorter, heavier or thinner, there are ways of creating the illusion of a different body size.

■ Shoulder/hip proportion

Visually compare the width of your shoulders to that of your hips. A man's shoulders are usually wider than his hips. If your shoulders extend unusually far beyond your hipline, however, you may appear top-heavy. You will also look unbalanced if your hips are equal to or wider than your shoulders.

The Three Body Types

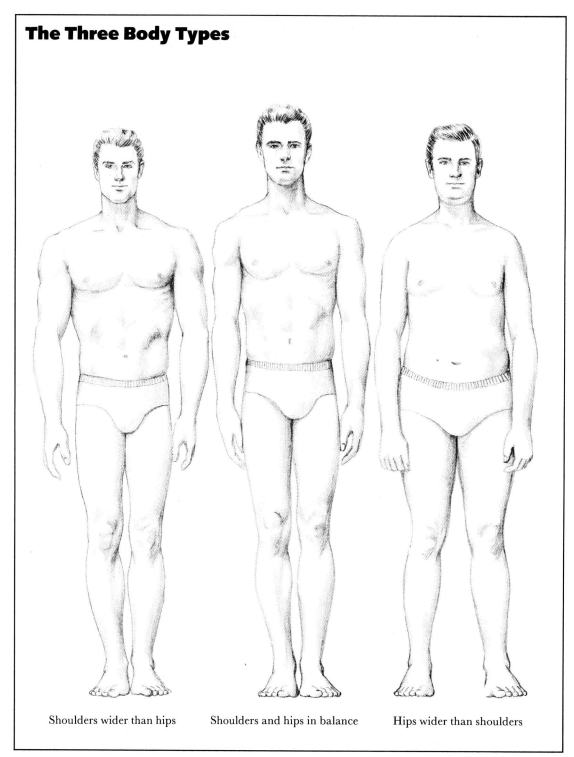

Shoulders wider than hips   Shoulders and hips in balance   Hips wider than shoulders

YOUR BODY PROPORTIONS

■ Shoulder slope

Facing forward, look at the slope of your shoulders. The average person has a five-centimetre (two-inch) drop from the base of the neck to the outer edge of the shoulder. If you have less than this drop, you have square shoulders; more, and your shoulders are tapered. Check also to see if one shoulder is markedly higher than the other.

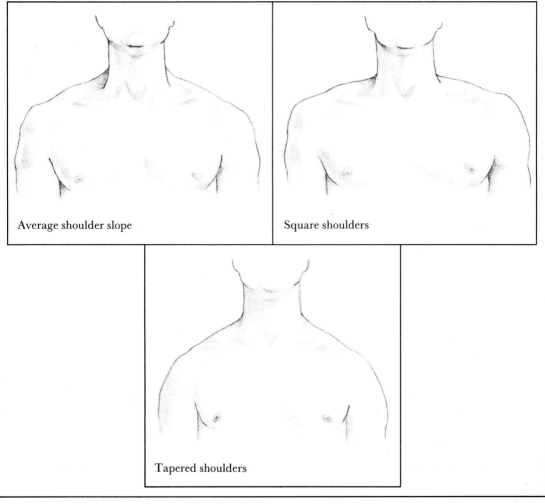

Average shoulder slope

Square shoulders

Tapered shoulders

■ Leg/torso proportion

In a perfectly proportioned body, the legs make up half of the total height. Measure the length of your leg from hip joint to floor. (If you have trouble locating your hip joint, just lift your leg. Where your trouser breaks at the hip is the joint.) Compare the length of your leg to your overall height to determine if your legs are short, long, or in proportion. Two centimetres (about an inch) either way is still considered average.

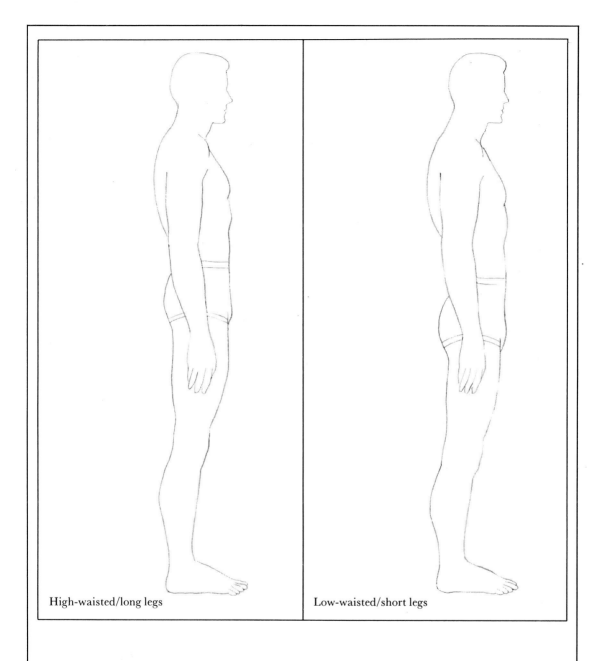

High-waisted/long legs

Low-waisted/short legs

■ Waist/body proportion

First look at your total height, then look at your waistline (when belted). Does your waist seem especially high or low, or does it strike a pleasing proportion to your height? Many people with long legs tend to be high-waisted; short legs often contribute to a low-waisted look.

■ Neck

See if your neck is very short or very long. Anything in between is not a problem. If you have a double chin, or if your chin or jowls rest against your collar, you need to compensate for your short neck. You can also camouflage a very long neck by making small adjustments in collar fit.

■ Arms

Your arms are of average length if, when they hang loosely at your sides, the bottom knuckle of your fist is parallel to your crotch. Check also to see if one arm is longer than the other.

■ Upper back

Stand sideways to the mirror and check the profile of your shoulders and upper back. Is your posture relatively straight or is your upper back rounded with your shoulders tilted forward?

■ Bottom

While standing sideways to the mirror, check the profile of your seat. Especially flat or prominent buttocks require special attention.

Solutions

Now that you know which areas of your body require special consideration, it's time to focus on the clothing lines and details that will bring your total look into balance. Some of this information will be covered in greater detail later in this book, but here's an introduction to how to achieve a perfectly balanced look for your body.

■ Height/weight

If you want to look taller, add vertical lines. Consider a three-buttoned suit made of solid or pinstriped material rather than a plaid, check or tweed fabric, which tends to add width. In casual wear, you are best in a monochromatic look – perhaps navy trousers with a navy sweater. A jacket, sweater or shirt that contrasts sharply with your trousers will simply cut you in half. Corduroy, with its vertical ribs, is a good choice in casual trousers. To continue an unbroken line to the floor, wear trousers without turn-ups with only the slightest break over the shoe, and match or at least blend shoe and trouser colour.

If you are too thin, you can look heavier with clothes that add bulk and make use of horizontal lines. Create width in suits by adding some padding to the shoulders and by choosing tweeds and plaids or checks. Avoid three-button suits and heavily waisted coats, which are slimming. If the look suits you, consider wearing widely spaced double rear vents and a double-breasted coat. Sweaters with horizontal stripes are excellent choices for leisure wear. You are the lucky individual who can wear layers of clothing. Try a T-shirt or turtleneck light sweater under your usual shirt.

If you want to minimise your height, horizontal lines can divide the length of your body into segments and make you appear shorter. A dark jacket or sweater with lighter trousers is an excellent way to make yourself look shorter. In suits and jackets, patterns are better than solids. Trousers with turn-ups and prominent breaks can also make you look shorter. Consider wide belts and large buckles or colourful cloth belts with casual wear to provide a strong horizontal line.

To appear slimmer, choose vertical lines that lengthen and narrow your body. Suits with vertical stripes or those solid fabrics are excellent choices. Avoid wide double-breasted suits as well as those with natural shoulders and no nipped-in waist. (A double-breasted suit with buttons placed closer together can be slimming.) A crisp shoulder line and vertical darts in your suits will remove some weight. Heavy tweeds and bulky handmade sweaters will add weight, but trim sweaters with set-in sleeves and V necks will make you look slimmer.

■ Shoulder/hip proportion

If your shoulders are too broad for your hips, you need to add dimension below the waist. Suit coats with pocket flaps and casual jackets with patch pockets will add needed width. Avoid peaked and extremely wide lapels, which tend to emphasise shoulder width. When selecting trousers, look for pleats, on-seam pockets, and bulky or heavy fabrics. Trim sweaters with raglan sleeves will also reduce apparent shoulder width and help create a more balanced look in casual wear. Avoid boat neck pullovers, as this wide, shallow neckline increases apparent shoulder width.

If you have hips that are equal to or wider than your shoulders, emphasise the shoulder and chest area. Add some padding to the shoulders of your suits. When possible, select

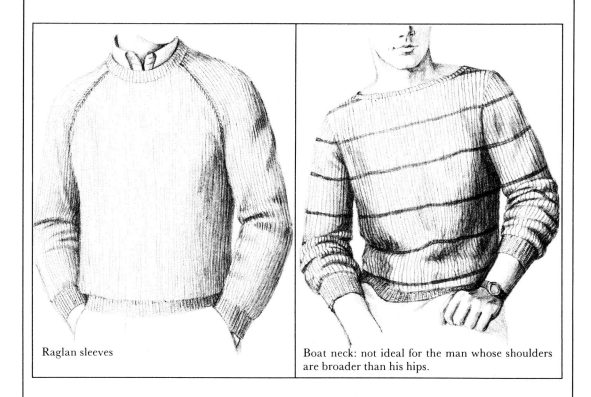

Raglan sleeves

Boat neck: not ideal for the man whose shoulders are broader than his hips.

lapels that point upward and outward. Avoid trousers with pleats and on-seam pockets; slanted pockets produce a trimmer look. To add width to the shoulders, wear sweaters and shirts with set-in sleeves and fit them so that the shoulder seams extend slightly beyond your natural shoulder. In casual wear, draw attention upward by combining brightly coloured shirts and sweaters with dark slacks. Sweaters and cotton knit shirts with horizontal stripes across the chest and shoulders are ideal.

■ Shoulder slope

*If your shoulders are tapered,*you can make them appear squarer by slightly padding suit shoulders and by choosing, when possible, lapels that point upward. In sweaters and cotton knit shirts, set-in rather than raglan sleeves will add definition to your shoulders.

YOUR BODY PROPORTIONS

Soften the angles of very square shoulders by avoiding padding. Suits and jackets with natural shoulders are excellent choices. Extremes of lapel width – either wide or narrow – tend to emphasise the shoulder area and call attention to shoulder shape. Lapels or shirt collars that point somewhat downward will also divert attention away from very square shoulders. In sweaters and cotton knit shirts, raglan sleeves and V necks may help to create the illusion of a more tapered shoulder line.

■ Leg/torso proportion

To shorten very long legs visually, wear trousers with turn-ups and a prominent break. Wearing a slightly longer suit jacket and selecting slacks with a shorter distance from crotch to waistband may also help diminish apparent leg length. Two-button or single-button jackets offer your best proportions. Wear your belts as low as possible, and choose contrasting colours for your shirts and trousers.

If your legs are short, you can add length by avoiding turn-ups and by hemming trousers at a length that produces only a slight break in the trouser leg over the shoe. Wearing the crotch of your pants as high as is comfortable and shortening your suit jackets slightly will also help create the illusion of longer legs. A three-button suit adds apparent length to your legs as well.

■ Waist/body proportion

A high waist can be camouflaged by trousers with a short distance from crotch to waistband because the belt will sit low on your waist. Sweaters worn over trousers and slightly longer suit jackets will also help create the illusion of a lower waistline. However, pleated trousers should be avoided, as they draw unwanted attention to a high waistline. Casual belts that match or blend with shirt colour lengthen the upper body.

A low waist can be made to appear higher by wearing trousers that have a long distance between crotch and waistband. Wide waistbands and belts that match trousers in colour can also visually raise the waist. Wearing cotton knit shirts or perhaps even sweaters tucked into the waistband will also raise the midline.

■ Neck

To disguise a long neck, look for shirt collars that fit high on the neck. Crewneck sweaters and turtleneck shirts are good choices for your casual wardrobe. Avoid open V necks.

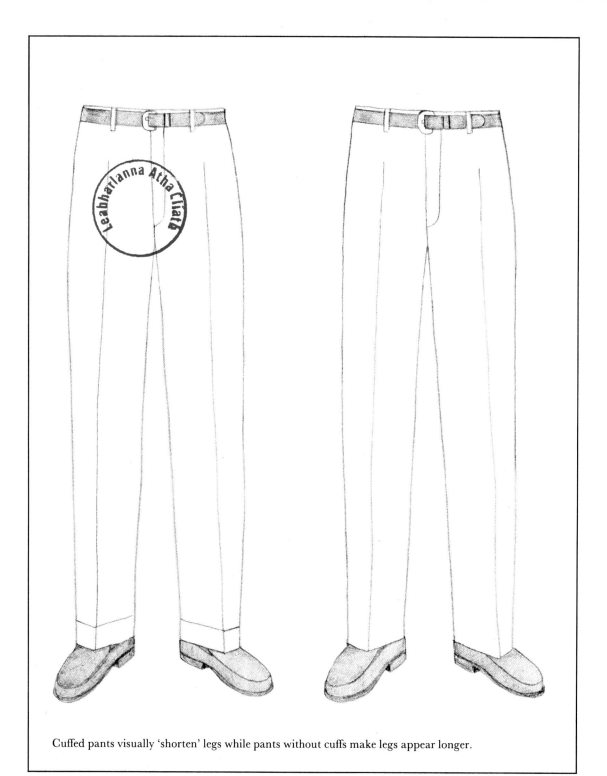

Cuffed pants visually 'shorten' legs while pants without cuffs make legs appear longer.

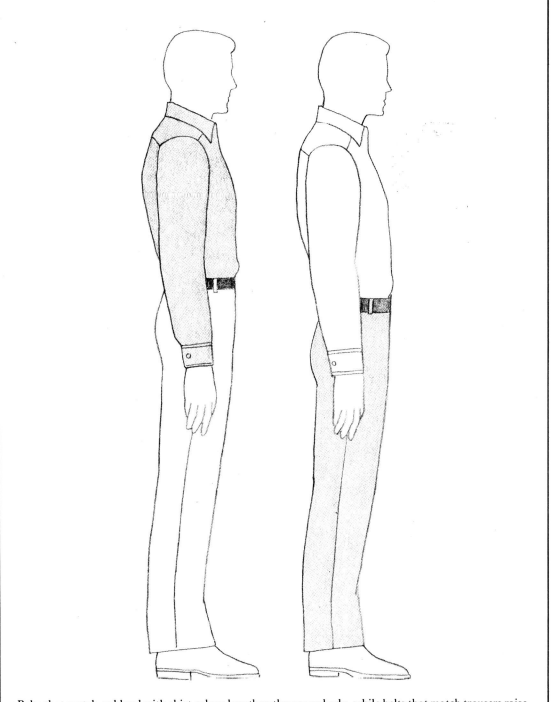

Belts that match or blend with shirt colour lengthen the upper body, while belts that match trousers raise the waist.

A short neck will appear longer when you wear V neck sweaters and open collared shirts. In dress shirts, choose styles with low-fitting collars.

Suits and coats will also have to be specially altered to lower the collar. Avoid crewnecks and turtlenecks.

■ Arms

If you have short arms, lengthen suit jacket sleeves slightly so that a bit less than the usual amount of shirt cuff shows. Also reduce the distance between the hem of the sleeves and the bottom of the jacket by shortening the jacket hem slightly. Suits and jackets cut with high armholes and raised padded shoulders visually lengthen arms. Sweaters and knit shirts with raglan sleeves may also lengthen arms by providing an unbroken line from collar to cuff.

If you have long arms, allow a bit more shirt cuff to show. Any cuff visually shortens your arm. Lengthen your jacket slightly. Elbow patches may also help to break up a long arm line. In casual wear, cotton knit shirts and sweaters with stripes on the upper arms help to create balance.

■ Upper back

With a rounded back, you do best to select suits in solid colours, since tailoring the jacket to fit your back often distorts the fabric's pattern at the centre back seam, accentuating the roundness. (Pinstripes that have been bowed into a barrel shape greatly emphasise a round back.) Sweaters with horizontal stripes help to camouflage your posture, but collarless shirts make it appear more pronounced.

■ Bottom

If you have a prominent bottom, compensate by selecting suit jackets with a single centre vent. If you need a high vent to provide extra room, make sure it lies flat. Wearing sweaters out over your trousers will create a smooth line from shoulder to bottom. Be careful not to let your sweater ride up in the back, making you look swaybacked.

If your bottom is flat, wear jackets with slightly nipped waists and double vents. Trousers must fit flawlessly to avoid a droopy look. For casual trousers, corduroys are better than tight jeans.

CHAPTER EIGHT

YOUR SUIT: SIZE, CUT, FIT AND QUALITY

For most men a suit represents a major investment. A quality suit makes a strong statement about you – your lifestyle, personal credibility, career goals. Choosing a suit in your seasonal palette is only half the mission. In addition, the suit must fit properly.

Clothes can't make the man unless they fit the man! As we have learned, some men are broad-shouldered and narrow-hipped, others have a long line that doesn't vary much from head to toe, while others are long-legged, high-waisted or square-shouldered. Depending on your build, you'll need a suit cut to fit your body type in order to be well dressed.

Understanding how to fit your body is not difficult. After reading this chapter, you'll know whether a suit fits you or not.

DETERMINING YOUR SUIT SIZE

When shopping for a suit, have the salesperson determine your jacket size by measuring around your chest at its widest point (usually under your armpits). If your arms are heavy or muscular and out of proportion to your chest, you will probably need to buy a bigger size.

Next, measure your waist – over a shirt, but not over trousers – at the point where you normally wear a belt, usually a little below your natural waist. In determining your suit size, always fit the jacket first, for it is easier and less expensive to alter trousers than it is to adjust a jacket.

Recheck your size each year; don't keep asking for the same size out of habit. As you gain or lose weight or grow older, your suit size will change.

Working out whether you need a short, an average or a long fitting needs a little care. Generally, 'short' fits men who are under 173 cm (5 ft 8 in), average are for men 173 cm to 182 cm (5 ft 8 in to 6 ft) and longs are for men over 182 cm (6 ft). All these sizes and lengths vary in every dimension, including jacket length and sleeve length.

Your height is not the only factor to consider when deciding what length you need for a suit; arm length and the relationship between torso and leg length are just as important. A man who is 170 cm (5 ft 7 in) tall may need an average suit if his torso and arms are long.

Men on the borderline between two sizes need to try on several suits and compare fit according to the principles presented later in this chapter.

DETERMINING WHICH CUT IS BEST FOR YOU

Size is one factor, cut is another. In order to get the best fit, you should match the cut of the suit to your body build.

Dress appropriately when shopping for a suit or having one fitted by a tailor. Wear a suit so you will have on a shirt, a tie and the proper shoes when trying on the new suit. Add all the things you usually carry in your pockets so the tailor can judge the fit correctly.

The standard shape

This suit has a slightly nipped-in waist with added vertical seams in the jacket to give shape and style. The lightly padded shoulders and crisper line are flattering to many body types. The standard shape has a single-breasted jacket, two buttons and a centre vent. It has flap pockets and a breast pocket. The trousers hang straight from the knee.

The slimmer line

The slimmer line generally has wider shoulders, with wider lapels. It is double breasted, and has three buttons. It has flap or jetted pockets on the jacket, and is usually worn with four pleat trousers, sometimes with turn-ups. This could be called the younger man's suit.

The standard shape

The slimmer line

FITTING YOUR SUIT

Now you know your size and have determined the cut that best fits your build and lifestyle, you need to have your suit carefully fitted.

Jacket

■ Shoulders

Check this area first to determine if the proper suit size has been chosen. The shoulders of a jacket are crucial to a good fit. The seam that joins the sleeve to the jacket should rest at the natural edge of your shoulders, neither hanging over nor being stretched by your arms. (If you have very large arms you may have to have your suits tailor-made.)

Before they will reset sleeves to adjust shoulder width, tailors generally recommend trying another jacket size and making other adjustments. Don't be surprised if you have to try on several suits. Another size or a suit from a different manufacturer may make a great deal of difference. If your shoulders are tapered, causing the jacket to bunch due to excess fabric, you can add shoulder pads to correct the problem. The pads will not only improve the fit of the jacket but will give your shoulders a more attractive line.

■ Chest

To check for proper chest fit, reach forward to determine if you can move freely. Look at the fabric between your shoulder blades and make sure it does not pull or wrinkle. Small adjustments can be made by taking in or letting out the centre back seam of the jacket. If the wrinkles tend to be diagonal, you probably have one shoulder higher than the other. Have a small pad built into the lower shoulder.

■ Collar

Very few man can buy a suit without having the collar raised, lowered, or shortened. Square or very tapered shoulders, a neck that is thin or thick, short or long and a rounded back all create special problems in collar fit.

Look in a three-way mirror. The jacket collar should hug the back of the neck with a small amount of shirt collar showing above it. If the shirt is hidden or there is a buckle of excess jacket fabric just below the suit collar, you need to have the collar lowered. This is done by removing excess fabric from the back of the jacket just under the collar.

If more than a small amount of the shirt collar is showing, the collar should be raised. Extra fabric is built into the collar in all better men's suits.

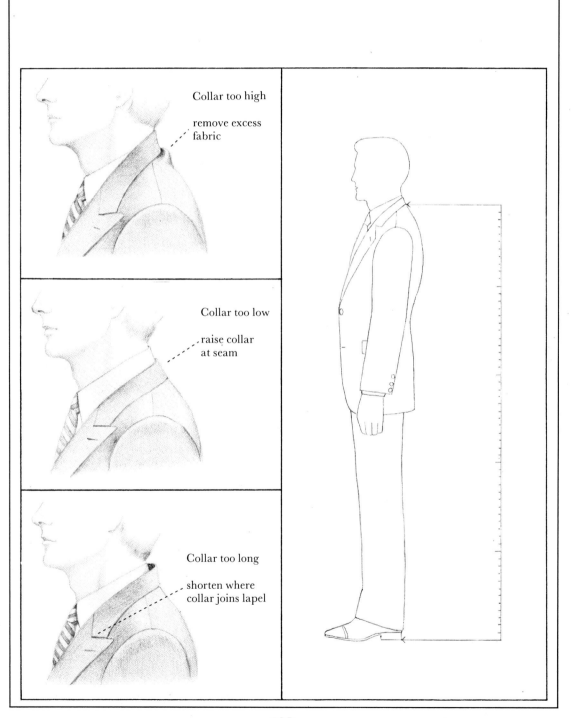

Collar too high

remove excess
fabric

Collar too low

raise collar
at seam

Collar too long

shorten where
collar joins lapel

If the suit collar pulls away from your neck or if the jacket lapels pull out or buckle, you need to take up the slack by shortening the collar. The collar is shortened at the notch where it joins the lapel in front.

■ Length

The proper length of a jacket is strictly a matter of proportion. An old rule of thumb was to stand with your arms at your sides, fingers curled under. If the hem of the jacket fell in the curve of the fingers, it was the right length. But this rule does not accommodate people with long or short arms, and you may end up looking unbalanced. Generally, your jacket should be long enough to cover your buttocks. If you have very long legs, however, you may want to wear your jacket slightly longer than your buttocks to make your legs appear shorter and more balanced. If your legs are very short, you'll want to wear your jacket just above the bottom of your buttocks in order to give the illusion of longer legs. Have the tailor measure you (with shoes on) from the lower edge of the suit collar to the floor, and divide the measurement in half. For a well-proportioned look, the bottom of your jacket at the back should fall approximately at that halfway point.

Jacket length should be even all around. Unbutton the jacket and check the bottom of the jacket closure. If the sides don't match evenly, you probably have one shoulder lower than the other. Build a pad into the lower shoulder instead of altering the jacket hem. Also, stand sideways in front of a mirror and compare the length of the jacket front and back. If you have rounded shoulders, you may need to lengthen the back of the jacket or shorten the front.

■ Vents

Button the jacket and check to see if the vent pulls open at the back. If it does, you need additional room in the waist and in the lower part of the jacket (the skirt). Have the side seams let out or the buttons moved, or both.

■ Torso

If you have excess material in the waist and hip area of the jacket, have the tailor take in the side seams and the back centre seam, or all three. If the waist is too tight or appears too pinched in for your taste, have the seams let out.

■ Sleeves

As a general rule, the hem of your sleeve should end just at the break of your wrist, covering your wrist bone, but leaving room to allow up to a centimetre or half an inch of shirt cuff to show. Make sure the tailor checks both sleeves. Most of us have one arm slightly longer than the other. Also, have the tailor check that the fabric in the upper portion of your sleeve isn't too snug or baggy. Sleeves should rest lightly on the upper arms without binding, and should hang smoothly when your arms are at your sides. If a sleeve has a diagonal wrinkle in the upper arm, your tailor will have to reset the sleeve and rotate it slightly. This alteration is expensive, and some tailors are unwilling to do it. If your tailor won't make this change, don't buy the suit. It will never look right.

Trousers

Try on trousers with a belt or braces and put your wallet in your back pocket if you normally carry it there. Check the fit in a three-way mirror so that you can see without twisting and throwing off the natural drape of the fabric. Complete all adjustments to waist, seat and thigh before marking length.

■ Waist

Determine proper waist size by having the tailor pin excess material at the back or, if your trousers are too small, by unbuttoning the waistband. Before marking the waist size, be sure that the trousers are resting where you want them on your hips.

If your hips and waist are close to the same measurement, your slacks may slip down all day, affecting the length. Wearing braces will alleviate the problem, and you'll be surprised at how much more comfortable you are.

If your waist is 23 cm (9 in) smaller than your jacket size, you'll probably need to have your suits tailor-made. You cannot successfully alter trousers that have so much drop from shoulder to waist with just a nip and tuck. Some shops will totally remake the trousers for you, completely take them apart and recut them, which is still cheaper than having a tailor-made suit.

■ Seat

Check seat fit by looking for wrinkling and sagging at the back (too large) or pulling, especially at the pockets (too small). Major adjustments in the seat generally require an accompanying alteration of the thighs. Always sit in trousers to check the fit; pulling may not be apparent until you are seated. While standing, try swinging your leg forward or taking a few steps. Binding at the knee is another indication that additional room is needed in the seat.

If the trousers don't rest evenly on your hipbones or if there are diagonal wrinkles at the crotch and thigh area, you probably have one hip higher than the other. An expert tailor may be able to reset the waistband to alleviate the problem.

■ Rise

If the pants extend above your waist or don't come up high enough, the rise is not right for you. Be sure that you have selected the correct suit size in terms of short, regular, or long. A trousers waist that is too low cannot be raised, and lowering the waist all around is an expensive alteration. A tailor-made suit may be the best option in extreme cases.

■ Legs

Turn sideways and look at the way the trousers hang. Legs should fall straight and centre evenly over each foot. Large calves will cause the trouser leg to pull back toward the heel. If you have prominent thighs, the fabric will bind over them when you bend or sit. Only limited alterations are possible in the thigh and calf areas. If this is a problem for you, you may need to reconsider the style of the suit you have chosen.

While standing, look down at each trouser crease. Ideally the crease should fall centred over the middle toe. If you have bow legs, the crease will fall over your little toe; if you are knock-kneed, the crease will fall over your big toe. Re-pressing the crease is not the answer to this problem; adjusting the side seams may be.

■ Length

Alterations to the waist, seat, thigh, and calf areas affect the way trousers hang and thus change the overall length. Have the tailor complete all other adjustments before marking length. If alterations to waist, seat, thigh, or whatever involve taking in material, trousers may be pinned to approximate the finished product, enabling the tailor to determine the proper length at the first fitting. If seams have to be let out, it is best to have the length marked at the second fitting.

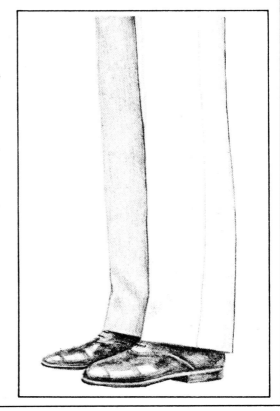

You must wear proper shoes to have the length of trousers marked. The hem of the trouser legs should clear the shoe heel and should rest on the front of the shoe with a slight break. The hem may be tapered so that the back hangs slightly longer than the front. Make sure that the tailor measures both legs, since one hip may be higher or one leg longer than the other.

Whether you finish trousers with turn-ups or plain bottoms is largely a matter of personal taste and of your desire to make your legs look longer or shorter. If you tend to wear out the back edge of your trouser turn-up, you can have the tailor sew in a heel stay (an extra layer of fabric) to extend the life of your trousers.

QUALITY OF SUIT CONSTRUCTION

The price of a suit depends partly on the amount of time that goes into its construction. Less expensive suits will reflect labour-saving short cuts. But even an expensive suit, while it may use first-class fabric, may occasionally cut corners on construction to keep the price down.

How do you recognise quality in a man's suit and avoid paying a premium price for a not-so-premium garment? Here are a few points to check when considering a suit.

■ Pattern
Check the side and back seams and make sure the patterns match. It requires handwork and more material to make the seams line up correctly. Lower-quality suits may skimp here.

■ Sleeve
The buttons on the sleeve should be placed so the edges just touch each other. A very expensive suit should have buttonholes that really work. Working buttonholes are rarely found on inexpensive garments.

■ Collar
Look at the stitching on the underside of the collar. Hand-sewn collars will be flat and hug the neck better. Look for close hand stitching.

■ Chest
The material that covers the chest (not including the lapel) has an inner lining to help the garment hold its shape. Squeeze the material over the chest and see if it is soft and resilient. If it's stiff, don't buy it.

■ Lining
Some jackets are fully lined, while others have lining only in the front and the top half of the back. Properly lined jackets have an expansion fold on the inside of the

hem. The lining should be folded under, neatly pressed, and sewn a little higher than the fold. If the fold is merely rolled under and not properly pressed, the lining will begin to droop and show beneath the hem.

FABRIC

Choose quality fabric. For the ideal in appearance, fit, and wear, choose a natural fibre, usually wool. You may want to have a small percentage of polyester blended with the wool, as polyester gives the cloth stamina and prevents wrinkles. Natural fibres, especially soft wools or linen, don't hold their shape well except in heavier weights or in jackets. *Never* buy a double-knit or all-polyester suit. Both look cheap and unsophisticated.

A suit in your colour made of quality fabric and fitted to perfection is essential to creating an image that brings out your best. Now let's complete the picture with shirts and ties that are just right for you, too.

CHAPTER NINE

YOUR SHIRT

Whether casual or dressy, your shirt is the most important item of clothing you wear because it is the colour closest to your face. In sportswear, your shirt may set the tone for your whole look. In business and dress shirts, you also have a tie and suit to work with, but your shirt is still the main body of colour close to your face.

In casual wear, there's no excuse not to look good. You can always find a colour that flatters from the wide offering of casual shirts now available. In dress shirts, it may be more difficult to find a specific colour, depending on your season. Look quickly through the shop, and if it doesn't carry your colour, move on. Another shop, another buyer, another designer, another manufacturer may give you what you're looking for.

THE COLLAR

The most noticeable aspect of a shirt, aside from its colour and overall quality, is the collar. The *style* of the collar, in addition to suiting your taste, must also suit the style of your other clothes as well as the occasion. The *shape* and *size* of the collar should be in proportion to your face. And of course the collar must *fit*. I will deal with fit in the last section of this chapter. Right now let's look at style, size, and shape.

The button-down collar is appropriate for business, as well as casual and informal social wear. It is not suitable for formal affairs. Button-downs tend to pull and wrinkle when worn with a tie. Make sure that yours are well fitted, that your tie is not too wide for the collar and that your shoulders don't pull the shirt fabric, creasing it across the top of your chest and pulling the collar out of line (move the buttons if necessary).

The standard collar comes in various sizes and shapes with points ranging from short and wide to long and thin. It is dressier than the button-down and suitable for business or social events. The standard collar has crisp, clean lines and looks best when lightly starched and pressed.

The full-spread collar has wide, shortish points that are spread far apart. It is always dressy. It suits those who have a special flair or formality in their personal style. It must be worn with a wide knot in the tie. The full-spread collar does not flatter a man with a wide face.

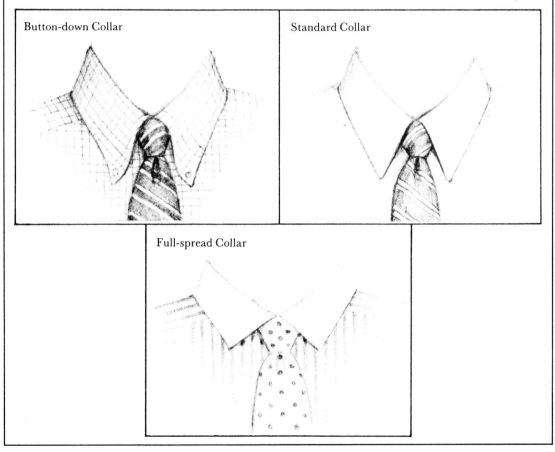

Button-down Collar

Standard Collar

Full-spread Collar

COLOUR FOR MEN

The *size* and *shape* of the collar that looks best on you are determined by the size of your head and body and the shape of your face. Ready-made shirts change some-what from year to year, according to fashion. Some styles are faddish and do little for most men. Big strapping men look pretty silly in the dinky little collars popular in the early 1980s. Always flatter yourself rather than compromise your looks to fashion. With subtle adaptations you can be in style and still wear becoming shirts that will last through many a trend.

If you have an oval face or one of average proportions, you can wear most collar styles and need only remember to scale them to your face and body size. If your face is long and thin or wide and round, you need to be more selective. The variety of collars available in ready-made shirts probably offers enough choice for most men, but some of you will want to invest in tailor-made shirts. Adjusting the height of your collar will do wonders for the appearance of your neck. Skilfully chosen, your collar can flatter your face and create the illusion of better propor-tions.

If you have a long, thin face, choose a collar of medium length that is a little wide. Avoid the very wide spread, as it is the extreme opposite of your face and will accentuate its thinness.

If you have a wide or round face, it can appear lengthened and slimmed by a slightly longer and thinner collar. An extremely long and thin collar is too badly out of balance with your face and will accentuate rather than minimise your problem. Avoid spreads, which accentuate wideness.

If you have a long neck, your collar should be slightly higher all round than the stan-dard cut. Adjust your suit-collar height as well.

If you have a short neck, choose a shorter collar to keep from looking stubby. Your suit-collar height should be proportionally adjusted, too.

If your neck is wrinkled, choose a collar higher in front.

If you have a very small or a very large head and face, your collar size should be scaled to your size: smaller collar for small head, larger for large head. In addition to being in flattering proportion to your face, the collars of your business and dress shirts must be compatible with the style of your suits and jackets and the shape of your jacket lapels. If you've chosen a slightly wide lapel to suit your face and body shape, don't select a thin, narrow collar. If you're wearing a narrow-lapelled casual jacket, don't accompany it with a wide spread shirt collar.

Wrong: Long, thin collar lengthens thin face

Right: Longer, thinner collar slims round face

Right: Medium width collar makes thin face appear fuller

Wrong: Average collar height exaggerates long neck

Right: Raised collar minimises long neck

Right: Lowered collar lengthens short neck

Wrong: Average collar height exaggerates short neck

Last, make sure your collars are clean, well-pressed and not worn out. A collar that is frayed around the edges will ruin your image. Shirts that are worn frequently become familiar old buddies. Take a look at yours and toss out the frazzled ones.

THE CUFF

Your cuff is important in creating a finished, well-groomed look. The length of your cuff is critical. Exposed wrists look just as bad as sleeves that are too loose and too long. Cuffs should be slightly longer than your jacket sleeves and should cover the wristbone.

For the neatest look in a cuff, make sure it fits your wrist trimly. A button on the placket above the cuff is the mark of a fine shirt. This look is found on expensive ready-mades or can be ordered on tailor-made shirts. If you choose a shirt that needs cuff links, make sure the formality of this style blends with your suit and is compatible with your personality.

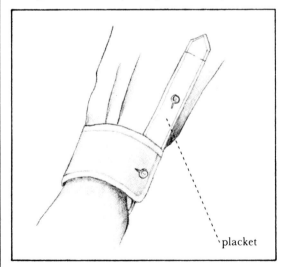

placket

Whatever style of cuff you choose, make sure it is crisply pressed, especially if the fabric is cotton. You can sometimes get away without pressing if your shirt is permanent press, but a stiff, lightly starched cuff gives a more finished look.

THE FABRIC

The best fabrics for dress and business shirts are 100 per cent cotton or cotton-polyester (wash and tumble dry) blends. A shirt of pure cotton looks great, fits, is cool, and takes colour well. However, it wrinkles – sometimes badly! – after a day at work. A permanent-press cotton-polyester blend (usually 65 per cent cotton/35 per cent polyester) may be the best choice for long wear.

In casual shirts you may choose from cottons, denims, corduroys, flannels, wools or knits. Take time to find the right colour, and select good quality that will wear well.

Forget 100 per cent synthetic fabrics for either business or casual wear. These fabrics almost always look cheap and don't 'breathe'. Silk shirts are strictly for evening wear or for the flashier professions where it is acceptable to dress up for work. Batiste or any see-through material is not appropriate for business, though it may be acceptable for summer wear.

PATTERNS

Patterns add interest to a shirt but are always less formal than a solid. The rule of thumb is that subtle patterns are suitable for business wear, and noticeable patterns are for casual or social attire. Most men are best advised to stay away from prints of any kind. Pictures, geometric designs and florals are seldom flattering.

Checks in subtle shades and small, well defined box checks can be acceptable for some professions. Checks are not a business look.

Some muted or bold checked shirts are generally suitable for leisure wear. Any bright, busy combination of colours is immediately casual.

When thin and crisp, stripes go with any style of business suit, even a pinstripe. As the stripes become wider or brighter, they are more sporty in appearance.

THE FIT

When selecting a ready-made shirt, you have only neck circumference and sleeve length to go by. If your arm length and neck size are not compatible with the standard size, you'll need a tailor-made shirt. In ready-mades you may also have to choose between an ill-fitting torso and an ill-fitting collar, since most manufacturers use a standard proportion of collar size to chest width. If you find yourself in this situation, choose an ill-fitting torso with a well-fitted collar, since the collar is the more visible. Some manufacturers do cut shirts fuller or slimmer, so ask the salesman which brand and designers are best for your build.

Fitting the collar

The collar's fit is crucial. If it is too tight, it will pull and wrinkle, so even the finest shirt will look poorly chosen. If the collar is too loose, you will look messy.

YOUR SHIRT

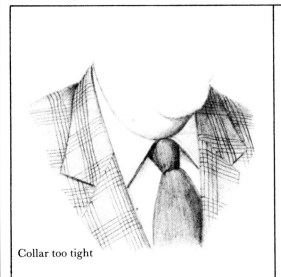

Collar too tight

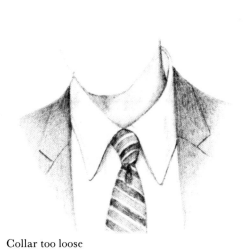

Collar too loose

Measuring sleeve length

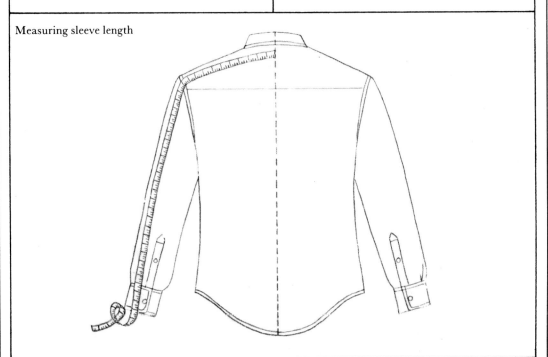

To measure your neck properly, measure around the lower part of your neck at the point where the collar button rests. The ends of the tape measure should touch, but the tape should not be pulled tightly. You want to have enough leeway so that a tie, when knotted, will not strangle you.

If your collar wrinkles when buttoned and worn with a tie, it is probably too tight. If you have square shoulders, your button-downs will wrinkle even if the collar size is correct. You may be able to adjust the buttons by moving them to a point where the collar doesn't pull. If that doesn't work, don't wear button-downs.

Recheck your collar size every year or any time you gain or lose weight. As you age, your neck size will change. My father was a surgeon who was more interested in his patients than his shirts. Year after year he ordered the same size shirts until one morning my mother found him with a razor, slitting the buttonhole on his brand-new shirt collars. 'What are you doing?' she cried. 'My shirt's too tight,' he replied. We wondered how many years he had been slitting his buttonholes instead of buying bigger shirts.

Fitting the cuffs and sleeves

Measure the length of your arm from the centre of the nape of your neck along your shoulder and down to your wristbone. If one is longer than the other, buy the length that fits your long arm and have the other sleeve shortened.

Your cuff should fit closely around your wrist but still be comfortable. Adjust the buttons if necessary. Some shirts come with two buttons sewn on so you can button whichever fits your wrist better. Remember, cuffs should not extend much below your jacket sleeve. By the same token, never settle for a sleeve that is too short.

If your arms are extremely broad or muscular, you may need a tailor-made shirt in order to build more fullness into the sleeve. Skimpy sleeves are not only uncomfortable but will also pull on the shirt yoke and make your collar wrinkle.

Fitting the shoulders

An ill-fitting shirt that is too tight will pull, creating long creases in the fabric across your collarbones. A shirt too loose in the shoulders will sag across the front.

If you have square shoulders, you'll need a square yoke or your collars will always pull and wrinkle. Square yokes have to be tailor-made, though some fashion designers cut a yoke that is more square than the standard.

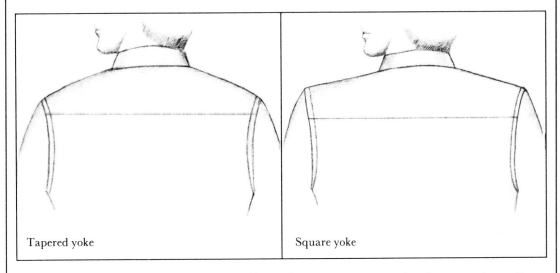

Tapered yoke

Square yoke

If your shoulders are quite tapered, you'll need an extra-tapered yoke – again, tailor-made. You may also need your collar shortened.

The taper of the shirt body is a matter of both comfort and looks. You want to avoid any pulling or constriction across your stomach, as well as any bunching up or bagging of surplus fabric. A trim, slightly loose line wears best and is most comfortable. Make sure the shirt is long enough to stay tucked in.

Try on different brands to see which are cut for you. Some designer shirts are slimmer through the torso. It is quite easy to put darts in a shirt that is too full, thus reducing the excess bulk.

Now you know everything you need to know to successfully buy and fit a shirt. When you find a shirt you really like, buy two, so you'll always have your favourite shirt clean and ready to wear.

Invest some time and effort in your shirt wardrobe – both casual and dress. A shirt in some form is one item of clothing you wear every day of your life.

CHAPTER TEN

YOUR TIE

Your tie can make or break your image. When chosen wisely, it brings colour to your face, style and class to your dress, and individuality to your business 'uniform'.

Yet many men shop for a tie as if it were to be worn by their shirt and suit alone. You will often see a man bring the suit and shirt to the counter and start trying the ties on the items of clothing, not thinking to try each tie on himself. I have often demonstrated to my clients how much – or how little – impact a tie has by having them try it on. The salespeople at better men's shops are quite used to seeing men standing in front of a mirror holding shirts and ties under their faces.

Naturally a tie must look good with your suit and shirt, but never at the expense of your face or personality. If possible, buy the suit first, then select the tie, and then choose a shirt to match both. The guidelines for co-ordinating jacket, shirt, and tie are in Chapter 11.

PATTERN

Each pattern has a different effect and is appropriate with different styles of suits and jackets. A useful tie wardrobe will include a sampling of patterns so that the look of any suit can be modified, making your clothes as versatile as possible.

Solid

Solids go well with solid suits, patterned jackets, and all shirts. They are versatile and can be either bold or conservative. Dark silk solid ties have a quiet elegance, while casual wools and knits bring either subtle or bright colour to your wardrobe without being busy or loud. Some solids have a same-colour pattern – a red-on-red

Solid

Solid

Rep (striped)

Rep (Striped)

Foulard

Club

Paisley

Plaid

stripe, for example. These are considered solids as long as the pattern is subtle. Silk solids have a sheen that adds richness to the tie, but stay away from very shiny or brocade versions.

Striped

Striped ties are based on the old regimental patterns. Stripes may be quite thin, of varying widths, or even and wide. Your selection will depend on your body proportions and personality. With clear-coloured suits, keep the stripes crisp; with suits in muted tones, the stripes should be softer.

Foulard

The term *foulard* was originally applied to a weave of fabric with a corded appearance. Today it is used for a tie pattern made up of a series of small, regularly spaced designs such as circles, ovals, diamonds or squares on a solid background. A foulard is often quite elegant. The small, subtle pattern brings colour to the tie without being loud.

Club

The club tie can be sporty or conservative. It has a regular pattern of club-like motifs – heraldic shields, sporting insignia, or animals – against a solid background. The pattern should be small, subtle, and not instantly recognisable. A tie with big, bold figures on it is *not* a club tie, and is generally considered tacky.

Check or Plaid

These ties are usually considered casual. In heavy wool they are appropriate in winter with tweeds and muted herringbone. They do not go with pinstriped suits or the sleeker worsteds. They can go well with flannel suits, however, and when made of linen or cotton, they go with summer suits as well. Just remember to avoid garish or loud checks at any time of year.

Geometric

Geometric ties cover everything from an enlarged diamond pattern to crisscross or vertically striped patterns. The large diamond shapes are more casual than the smaller versions, but either brings an angularity to your appearance – particularly flattering to the large man.

Dots

Dots range from polka dots to pin dots. Traditionally a very elegant tie, the polka dot is almost as versatile as the solid tie. Very small pin dots are even more formal, and are used for evening or with your more elegant business suits for special occasions.

Paisley

Paisley ties are useful because they combine so many colours that they mix and match well. In stronger colours paisley ties are too sporty for a business look, but when the colours and fabric are subdued, these ties can be elegant and dressy.

COLOUR

Your tie colour can enhance your face, add zip to your total appearance, and work as an accent to complete your outfit. It can also be a powerful tool for bringing an old wrong-colour suit into line. Always wear your right colour as the primary colour in the tie. Choose a patterned tie with a background colour from your chart and a design that brings in a small amount of the wrong colour from your suit. The tie will then blend harmoniously with the suit, while its primary colour offsets to some degree the suit's negative effect. Once your wardrobe has been changed over completely, however, try to buy only ties with your correct colours. There may be a touch of wrong colour in patterned ties, but the more visible the wrong colour is, the less it will do you justice.

Here are some guidelines for each season's ties.

Winter

Winters need clear, sharp colours. When shopping for a navy tie, be careful to buy a bright or dark navy rather than a muted one. Winters look excellent in solid colours, since a pattern can diminish the contrast or sharpness of the tie under a Winter's face. Solid dark blue-reds are especially flattering. Any patterns should contain some brightness or contrast. Best prints for the Winter man are stripes with sharp contrast (the width of the stripes depends on your body scale, face size, and personality). Second best are ties with repeat patterns if they contain some element of brightness or contrast. A tiny white diamond, for example, is better than a muted blue diamond. Geometrics are good for Winters. Polka dots are fine as long as they are sharp and suit your personality. Checks and plaids are rarely appropriate for a Winter, since a check or plaid that offers enough contrast is usually too loud for business wear. Paisleys are similarly problematic, but are occasionally all right if carefully selected. If the paisley is subtle, you must wear a pure white or a very icy shirt to provide the sharpness your look needs. A club tie is not your most exciting look. Wear it only if you are sentimental about the emblem.

Summer

Summers should choose more subtle ties in shades slightly more muted than Winter's. A Summer's best print is the repeated patterned tie, especially when the pattern is in a rounded shape such as a teardrop or oval. Summers should wear stripes that offer minimal contrast or look blended (either thin or wide, depending upon body scale, face size and personality). Checks or plaids are all right as long as they are blended. Dots are fine, too, as long as they are fairly small and not too sharp. Few Summers wear paisleys, but if they suit you, keep the pattern subtle and blended. Clubs are fine if the insignia is not too bright and the motif is conservative.

Autumn

The Autumn man needs richness in the colours of his ties. Often he has no cheek colour, and he depends upon that tie to brighten his face. Most Autumns look excellent in patterned ties, especially rich paisleys. Checks or plaids are great as well, particularly in combination with Autumn's tweeds and herringbones. Irregular stripes are also good, though ties with evenly spaced stripes of equal width may be too contrived and controlled for an Autumn man. Polka dots may also be too formal for you. Patterned ties are fine in almost any pattern as long as the scale suits your face and body size. Sporty club ties are good for Autumns.

Spring

Springs, like Winters, depend on clear colours, so their ties should never look dull or washed out. The Spring man wears solids well, usually in ties with a matt (non-shiny) finish. The best prints for Springs are casual, subtle plaids, widish stripes with medium contrast, and almost any foulard pattern. Severe stripes are too sharp for most Spring men, and polka dots are usually too formal. Sporty club motifs are good for Springs. A paisley will work only if it is carefully chosen in your colours. In general, it is not Spring's best look. Most geometrics are too severe for Springs.

YOUR TIE

WINTER

Solid	Excellent for contrast. Choose clear, sharp colours, especially in navy or red.
Striped	Excellent. Choose sharply contrasting stripes.
Patterned	Select patterns with brightness or contrast.
Club	Personal choice. Insignias better than sporty motifs.
Check or Plaid	Seldom appropriate.
Geometric	Excellent.
Dots	Choose sharp polka dots with high contrast.
Paisley	Seldom appropriate. Choose sophisticated neutrals rather than bold colours

SUMMER

Solid	Good in muted shades, medium to dark.
Striped	Good with blended stripes, subtle contrast.
Patterned	Excellent, especially when pattern is in a rounded shape such as teardrop.
Club	Personal choice. Avoid anything too bright.
Check or Plaid	Subtle patterns are good.
Geometric	Subtle rather than bold.
Dots	Dots are fine, usually small and not too sharp.
Paisley	Seldom appropriate but all right if soft and blended.

AUTUMN

Solid	Good in rich colours.
Striped	Good in irregular stripe.
Patterned	Almost any pattern.
Club	Sporty club motifs are fine.
Check or Plaid	Excellent, especially with tweeds and herringbone.
Geometric	Probably too formal.
Dots	Probably too formal.
Paisley	Excellent.

SPRING

Solid	Good in clear colours, never dull or washed out.
Striped	Choose medium-contrast stripes.
Patterned	Almost any pattern.
Club	Sporty cluf motifs are fine.
Check or Plaid	Excellent in casual, subtle colours.
Geometric	Probably too severe.
Dots	Probably too formal.
Paisley	Seldom appropriate.

YOUR TIE

FABRIC

A tie is never as effective – even one in the right colour and pattern – if it is made of a cheap fabric. Both the surface and drape of the fabric are important. Silk, fine wool, linen (for summer), and cotton are the best fabrics. Not only do good fabrics take colour better, but they also knot better than cheaper ones.

Generally any matt or flat-finish fabric can be worn for business, dress or casual occasions. Rougher textures are always more casual. A subtle sheen on silk is elegant in business wear and can be quite fancy. Shiny polyester can give a lively look.

WIDTH

The width of ties varies somewhat according to fashion, but the most flattering width for all men is between 8 cm and 9 cm (3 to 3½ inches) at the tie's broadest point. If you are broad-chested, you'll want a broader tie. If you are thin, choose narrower ties.

In addition, you need to have the tie in proportion to your collars. Here, too, a subtle difference, not a large one, bespeaks style.

LENGTH

The length of your tie should always be the same. When it is tied properly, the tip of your tie should hit just at the top of your belt. You will need to adjust the length when tying it. Depending upon your height, you will need more or less fabric to achieve this.

KNOTS AND BOW TIES

How you wear the tie is as important as the tie itself. There are three standard knots; each is suitable with different shirt collars and your overall body proportions. The tie knot should lie comfortably between your collar points with no gaps on either side and no pinching or crowding. Both wide-faced and thin-faced men should avoid very thin or very wide knots, which accentuate any proportion problems by either repeating the line or offering too extreme a contrast.

The following illustrations are drawn in mirror image, so you can prop the book up facing you while you stand in front of the mirror.

Tie length

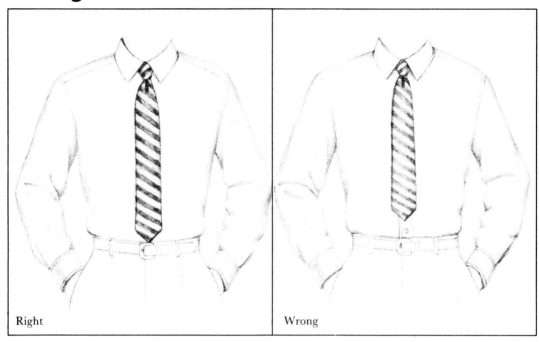

Right

Wrong

Tie width

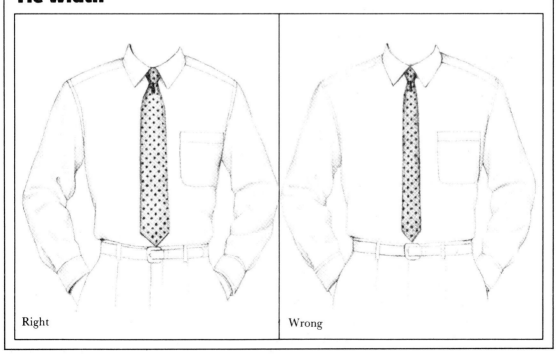

Right

Wrong

The Basic Knot

The basic knot is a longish knot and is proportioned for the button-down collar or the standard collar of average spread. Because this knot gives a longer finished tie, it is excellent for the tall man who needs a little more length.

1. Place the wide end of the tie on your right so it hangs about 30 cm (12 in) longer than the narrow end.
2. Wrap the long end around the short end and then behind, finishing on the right.
3. Continue to cross long end over short end, finishing on the left.
4. Pull long end through loop from the back.
5. Slip point through front of knot and tighten.
6. While pulling down short end with one hand, use other hand to slide knot up snugly.

The Half Windsor

The half Windsor is more triangular and is also proportioned for the standard collar.

1. Place the wide end of the tie on your right so it hangs about 30 cm (12 in) longer than the narrow end.
2. Wrap the long end behind the short end, finishing on the right.
3. Thread long end through loop and pull down to the left.
4. Cross long end over knot.
5. Pull long end through loop from the back.
6. Slip point through front of knot and tighten. While pulling down short end with one hand, use other hand to slide knot up snugly.

The Windsor

The Windsor knot is wide and triangular and is specifically for any shirt collar with a widish spread.

1. Place the wide end of the tie on your right so it hangs about 30 cm (12 in) longer than the narrow end.
2. Cross the long end over the short end and pull up through loop from the back.
3. Bring long end down and wrap behind short end, finishing on the right.

The Four-in-Hand

The Half Windsor

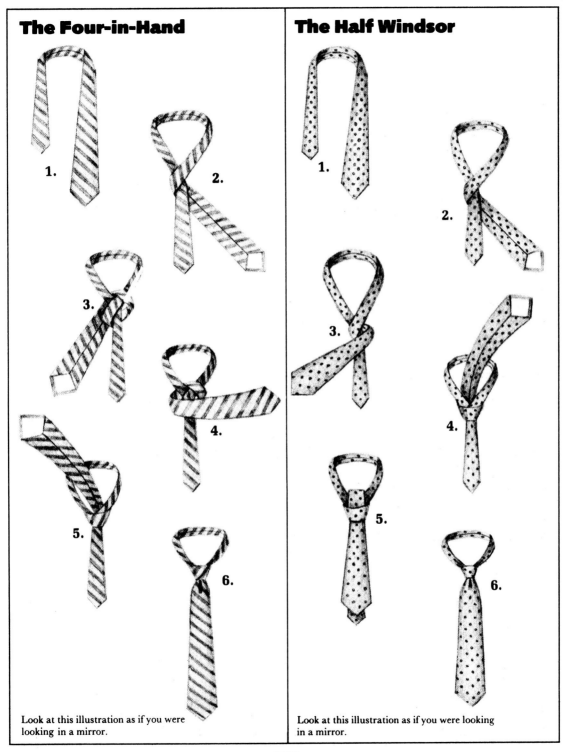

1.
2.
3.
4.
5.
6.

Look at this illustration as if you were looking in a mirror.

Look at this illustration as if you were looking in a mirror.

The Windsor

The Bow Tie

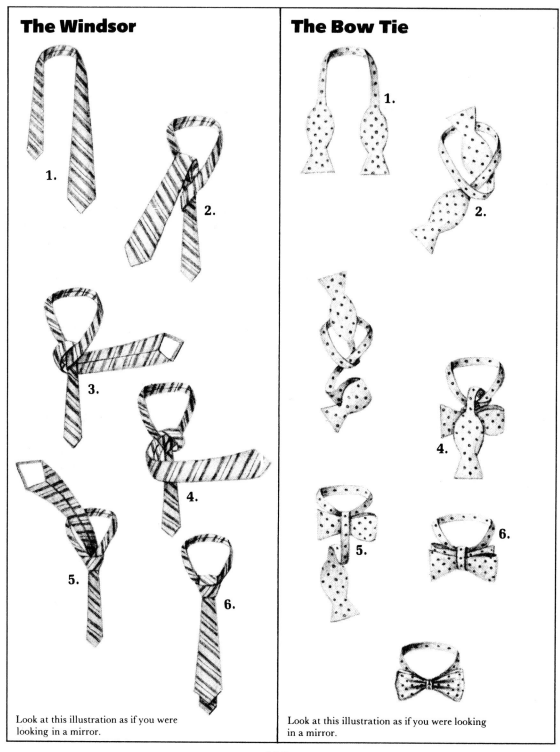

Look at this illustration as if you were looking in a mirror.

Look at this illustration as if you were looking in a mirror.

4. Thread long end through loop, then pull down and wrap across front of knot.
5. Thread through loop again.
6. Slip point through front of knot and tighten. While pulling down short end with one hand, use other hand to slide knot up snugly.

The Bow Tie

Wearing the bow tie is a matter of personal choice. But in all but formal attire, it is less serious or businesslike. The same thought and care should be given to the selection of its colour, pattern, and fabric as for the standard tie. Avoid clip-ons, even with a dinner jacket.

If you are going to wear a bow tie, here's a simple way of making a neat bow.

1. Pull left end to extend 4 cm (1½ in) below right end.
2. Cross long end over short end and pull up through loop from the back. Pull tight.
3. Fold short end to form front loop of bow.
4. While securing front loop with left hand, pull long end down across loop centre.
5. Loop long end around right forefinger toward chest.
6. Push new loop through knot behind first loop. Pull tight and adjust evenly.

Now read on to find out the best ways to successfully put your coat, shirt, and tie together. Although each is important separately, your overall image depends on how well you combine them.

CHAPTER ELEVEN

CO-ORDINATING JACKET, SHIRT AND TIE

Using your seasonal chart and the guidelines in this chapter, you can combine your suits and jackets with shirts and ties with minimal effort and maximum impact.

The approach to putting your clothes together is always the same. Think of your suit as your basic building block. It establishes the overall colour, style and look you are aiming for. Your shirt can be your white or any light colour in your palette that is compatible with the suit and the occasion. Your tie must then relate to the shirt colour, the suit colour or both.

With those principles in mind, follow these dos and don'ts to enjoy the pleasure of putting yourself together with grace and impact.

DO: BUY ONLY COLOURS FROM YOUR CHART

Using the Colour for Men system, blending suits or jackets with your shirts and ties will be more fun and much easier than ever before. All your clothes will go together because they are in compatible colours of your season and because you will buy shirts and ties that work interchangeably with your suits. If you have suits in the wrong colours, you may have to purchase a few compromise ties until you are able to phase out the suit (and the tie!). But once your wardrobe has completed its transition, don't buy anything *new* in a wrong colour.

DO: COMBINE THREE SOLIDS

Wearing a solid-colour shirt, suit, and tie is perfectly acceptable and a sure way to look good. This is *not* a boring look if the colours are compatible and look good on you. It is low-key, suitable for business, but also elegant.

Although all three clothing items are solids, you are actually combining only two colours, or two colours plus one neutral. Here are some rules for combining three solids tastefully and effectively.

■ If your shirt is your season's white, pale grey, or beige (i.e., pale neutral), your suit and tie may be two distinctly different colours. Usually your tie will be the accent colour. In casual wear the same principle applies, as long as the trousers are grey, beige/tan or your white.

Here are examples, by season, of combinations of three solids with a neutral shirt and two distinct colours, using the tie as accent.

Winter   Navy suit, white shirt, blue-red tie

Summer   Navy suit, soft white shirt, burgundy tie

Autumn   Navy suit, oyster shirt, rust or bittersweet red tie

Spring   Navy suit, ivory shirt, light rust tie

■ If your shirt is a colour (blue, pink, etc.), two of the three clothing items must be from the same colour family. A colour family is a series of tints or shades of the same colour. Light blue and navy are both from the blue family. Pink and burgundy are from the blue red family. Peach and rust are from the orange red family. Other same-colour combinations are beige and brown, buff and golden brown, ivory and camel, grey and black, salmon and tomato red.

Here are examples, by season, of combinations of three solids in which the shirt is a colour and the tie is in the same colour family as either the shirt or the suit.

Winter   Navy suit, icy pink shirt, bright burgundy tie (tie and shirt are from the same colour family)

Summer   Blue grey suit, light blue shirt, navy tie (tie and shirt are from the same colour family)

Autumn   Coffee brown suit, peach shirt, brown tie (tie and suit are from the same colour family)

Spring   Tan-coloured suit, peach shirt, light rust tie (tie and shirt are from the same colour family)

Right: Patterned suit, solid shirt, patterned tie.

Right: Patterned suit, patterned shirt, solid tie.

Wrong: Never combine three patterns.

DO: COMBINE TWO SOLIDS WITH ONE PATTERN

The second surefire look is created by combining two solids or semi-solids with one pattern. A semi-solid is a pattern that is so subtle that it gives the appearance of being solid. This can include a suit with a pattern that fades into the overall background or a tweed that is so closely woven with non-contrasting colours that the eye perceives it as solid.

If you choose a patterned tie, it must pick up the suit colour, the shirt colour or both colours.

Your tie must have some reasonable relationship to the colour of your suit or your shirt, preferably both. The most common error is choosing a tie that doesn't relate to both items or, sometimes, even to one. For best results, try to pick a tie pattern that repeats the suit colour and the shirt colour. If that's not possible, then repeat at least one. It's all right to have a few extra colours in the pattern as long as the suit and/or shirt colours are there.

In casual wear, your patterned tie may pick up the colour of the trousers instead of the shirt and/or jacket.

Here are examples, by season, of combining two solids with a patterned tie.

Winter   Navy suit, white shirt, navy, red, and white striped tie.

Summer   Navy suit, soft white shirt, small patterned tie with burgundy background and navy, soft white and medium blue pattern.

Autumn   Navy suit, oyster shirt, paisley tie in brown, blue, oyster white and beige.

Spring   Navy suit, ivory shirt, striped or tartan tie in shades of red, light blue, navy and ivory.

Note: Be sure to wear only *your* navy!

Here are examples, by season, of combining two solids with a patterned shirt.

Winter   Navy suit, red tie, dark blue and white hairline-striped shirt.

Summer   Navy suit, red tie, light blue and white striped shirt.

Autumn   Navy suit, bittersweet red tie, bittersweet and oyster white striped shirt.

Spring   Navy suit, rust tie, small check shirt in blue and brown.

If you choose a patterned shirt, it must pick up the colour family of either the suit or the tie.

The solid tie should not be the same colour as the solid suit unless it matches exactly, which is almost impossible. Do not wear navy colours that do not match.

If you choose a patterned suit containing threads of colour woven into the background, the tie must pick up a colour from the suit.

If you choose a monochromatic, patterned suit, the solid tie can be a different, contrasting colour.

If you choose a patterned jacket, the same principles apply for the shirt and tie. The solid trousers should pick up a colour from the jacket.

Here are examples, by season, of combining two solids with a patterned suit.

Winter	Charcoal grey pinstriped suit, white shirt, red tie.
Summer	Blue-grey suit with subtle burgundy threads, soft white shirt, burgundy tie.
Autumn	Brown and beige tweed suit, oyster shirt, bittersweet red tie.
Spring	Herringbone suit in golden brown, tan, and light beige, ivory shirt, brown or rust tie.

DO: COMBINE ONE SOLID WITH TWO NON-COMPETING PATTERNS

This combination is tricky because it leaves room for error. It is not as sure or easy as combining three solids, or two solids and one pattern. When done correctly, this combination subtly announces that you know your clothing. When wrong, alas, it loudly proclaims the opposite.

If you are unsure of your ability to recognise non-competing patterns, avoid putting two patterns adjacent to each other and you'll be safer. In other words, your shirt will be solid.

In casual wear, the same principles apply. Whether you choose a patterned jacket or patterned trousers, your second pattern will probably be your tie. The other two items will be solids.

The basic principles are:

Use a subtle pattern with a stronger one. Two subtle ones look washed out. Two bold ones are garish. A pinstriped shirt, which is subtle and evenly spaced, looks best if the tie has widish stripes rather than thin, evenly spaced stripes.

CO-ORDINATING JACKET, SHIRT AND TIE

Keep the lines of the patterns the same, or use one directional pattern with one all-over pattern. Because both checks and stripes have directional lines, they usually don't mix well with each other because the lines compete. However, a subtle stripe can mix with a bolder stripe or a subtle checked shirt can mix with a check or plaid because the lines are similar. Foulard, paisley, and club ties are all-over patterns, as are tweed, herringbone, tiny box checks, or very subtle checks in suits. These patterns can often mix with stripes or plaids. Two all-over patterns can mix as well, as long as one is subtle and the other stronger, or one is large and the other smaller.

Here are examples, by season, of combining a patterned suit or coat and tie with a solid shirt.

■ Pinstriped suit, striped, small patterned or dot tie, solid shirt.
■ Chalkstriped suit, heavier pattern in stripes, small patterned or dot tie, solid shirt.
■ Subtle business tweed or herringbone suit, striped or small patterned tie, solid shirt.
■ Heavy tweed jacket, wider-striped, ribbed knit, or club tie, solid shirt, solid trousers.
■ Wool houndstooth trousers; subtle striped or ribbed knit tie, solid shirt, solid jacket.

Here are examples of combining a patterned suit and shirt with a solid tie.

■ Pinstriped suit, subtle hairline-striped or soft striped shirt, solid tie.
■ Chalkstriped suit, subtle striped or thin-striped shirt, solid tie.
■ Tweed jacket, subtle checked shirt, solid tie.
■ Herringbone suit, pale striped shirt, solid tie.

Here are examples of combining a solid suit, patterned shirt, and patterned tie.

■ Solid suit, subtle hairline-striped shirt, striped or small patterned tie.
■ Solid suit, subtle striped shirt, irregularly wider-striped, small patterned, or club tie.
■ Solid suit, subtle plaid shirt, wider-striped check or plaid tie, or ribbed knit where the texture appears patterned.
■ Solid suit, subtle checked shirt, club tie.
■ Solid suit, white-on-white shirt, any patterned tie

Any patterned shirt that is *not* subtle should be worn with a solid tie.

DON'T: COMBINE THREE PATTERNS

There is no quicker way to ruin your image than to clutter yourself with too many patterns. You automatically draw the eye away from your face and call attention to the clothes. If you are very clever you may come up with some good pattern combinations, but they will look better on the hanger than under your face. Each pattern competes with the other and the eye has to move around trying to decipher the picture. Your impact is diminished.

DO: STRIVE FOR CONTRAST

It always looks best to have contrast between suit and shirt, shirt and tie. Think how boring a man looks in a grey suit, a white shirt and the same colour grey tie. But change that tie to red, navy, black, or even charcoal grey, and you have an entirely different impression.

There are two ways to create contrast: dark and light or light and bright. Some men need more contrast than others, depending on their season. A blue shirt with a medium blue tie offers medium contrast; a white shirt with a navy tie offers high contrast. The first is fine for Summers, the latter for Winters. All men need some degree of contrast to look exciting.

Contrast is the way to successfully pull off a monochromatic look. Mix a dark brown suit, beige shirt, and coffee tie – elegant. Even though the colours are all from the brown family, they offer varying degrees of intensity.

There are three basic combinations.

With a dark suit, wear a light shirt and a bright, medium or dark tie.

With a medium suit, wear a light shirt and a dark tie.

With a light suit, wear a medium shirt and a dark tie.

Winters, who cannot wear medium shirts, should wear a white or striped shirt and a dark or brightish tie.

DO: COMBINE COMPATIBLE FABRICS

Fabric varies in three ways: weight, texture, and finish.

The *weight* of a fabric depends on its content and the density of its weave. The year-round wools are medium and thinner. Lighter weights are thin and may be wool, cotton, linen, or blends.

Texture is determined by the rough weave of a fabric. Knits, tweeds and corduroys are heavily textured. Worsteds, tightly woven wools, fine cotton and silk are generally smooth in texture.

Finish has to do with the sheen of fabrics. Finishes range from such flat matt finishes as a flannel suit, cloth shirt or a wool tie to the high sheen in a silk tie.

When combining the weight, texture and finish of a coat or suit, shirt and tie, *keep likes with likes*. Heavy goes with heavyish, boucle goes with matt, smooth goes with a sheen. A tweed jacket (boucle matt finish) goes with a knit (matt finish) wool tie, and a solid worsted suit (smooth) with a silk tie (sheen).

Here are examples of appropriate fabric combinations.

■ A boucle tweed jacket, cloth shirt, a medium-weight textured knit tie.
■ A smooth worsted formal suit, a silk or fine cotton shirt, a silk tie.
■ A lightweight linen summer suit, either a cotton or cotton/polyester shirt, a cotton tie.
■ Corduroy trousers, a heavy flannel shirt.

With a lighter-weight, smooth-finish suit, it would be inappropriate to wear your heavy wool, loose-weave tie, even if the colour is right. The weight and texture are wrong. That suit may be worn with either a tightly woven lightweight wool tie or a silk tie.

DON'T: MIX STYLES OF CLOTHING

Clothing automatically has a style. It is dressy or casual, woodsy or executive, city or country, faddish or classic, depending on its colour, line, fabric and pattern. Obviously you would not wear a corduroy jacket with your pinstriped trousers. But there are subtler combinations that clash and ruin your image, too.

Colour that is bright tends to be sporty, casual or festive. Bright colours are only businesslike when used as accents, such as stripes in a tie. Pastels are fashion colours when worn in suits or jackets, but are conservative in business shirts. Dark colours are classic business and traditional country casual colours.

Patterns can be either conservative or sporty. Subtle patterns are classic, bold ones are sporty. Tartan, plaid, paisley and club tie patterns are sporty. Striped, polka-dot, and foulard patterns are more formal. However, some striped ties are casual and some paisleys are more formal, depending on their colours and their fabric.

Fabric is also dressy or casual. Knits and tweeds are sporty. Worsteds and silks are dressy. A silk shirt would never be worn with a knitted tie.

The *cut or styling line* of a garment determines a lot about its character. That is why a well-cut suit in a fine flat wool and conservative colour does *not* go with a cloth button-down shirt. The styles clash and so do the textures. The suit demands a clean line and a fine, smooth texture; the button-down has a chunky line and a rough texture.

SUMMARY

Here is a summary of the dos and don'ts of successfuly combining your coat, shirt, and tie.

Do Buy *only* colours from your chart.
Do Combine three solids.
Do Combine two solids with one pattern.
Do Combine one solid with two non-competing patterns.
Don't Combine three patterns.
Do Strive for contrast.
Do Combine compatible fabrics.
Don't Mix styles of clothing.

Now you know the rules for putting your clothes and your colours together, you are ready to begin refining your look and thinking about your personal style.

CHAPTER TWELVE

YOUR CLOTHING PERSONALITY

What is your clothing personality? As you go through life you begin to get a feel for what clothing styles really are *you*. Perhaps you long for the David Niven country gentleman look but your body and face call for the John Wayne image – rugged and casual. Maybe you feel you must have a pinstriped suit, but you never feel good in it and never receive compliments while wearing it. There is a reason for this.

To really look good, your clothes must reflect not only your inner spirit but also your physical self. Doesn't it make sense that your colouring, your build and your facial structure play a part in determining your best clothing image? Inner spirit counts, too, but not to the point where you spoil your natural qualities by trying to be something you are not.

You never have to wear anything that doesn't flatter you just to fit a mould. Whether you seek a social or corporate image, you can always dress appropriately without sacrificing your best look.

Your season gives you the first clue about your image because your colouring and the colours you wear automatically make a statement. In general, a Winter looks best in solid colours, sharp contrasts and a crisp silhouette – a rather formal look. A Summer man is more flattered by gentler contrasts, subtler patterns and slightly softer fabrics. The Autumn man, with his warm colouring, looks especially good in tweeds, checks and rich, rough fabrics, sophisticated but casual, while Spring is best in informal, relaxed clothing, also textured but always youthful, with colourful striped or checked shirts and ties.

But what if you are a Winter with light brown hair, blue eyes, a slight build and boyish face? You may *not* look your best when dressed in formal suits with boldly striped ties. If you are a tall, slim Spring with elegantly refined facial features and smooth, white-blonde hair, you are more formal and sleek than the casual Spring man described above.

So you need to take into consideration not only your seasonal colouring but also your size, body structure and facial features.

CLOTHING TYPES

Clothing images are not absolute and they may overlap, but depending on your individual personality, lifestyle and work environment, you can use them to influence your clothing selections in order to look and feel your best.

Dramatic

You are a man of *design, style, detail* and *sharp contrasts*. The dramatic man is authoritative, innovative, assertive. Everything about his appearance makes a bold statement; his clothes are of the latest fashion but not faddish.

The man who can wear dramatic attire is usually tall and lean, sometimes very thin, with broad, horizontal shoulders. Your body tends to have long, vertical lines rather than a chunky look, and your hair is dark or strikingly blonde or grey. Nothing about you is middle-of-the-road. You have angular facial features, perhaps a sharply pointed nose or chin and an angular body. You have a certain elegance about you, and walk with long strides and a confident air. You have built-in authority by virtue of your size and striking colouring. Your looks call for you to dress with authority, sophistication and a degree of formality. In general, you wear bold or dark colours mixed with your season's white for maximum contrast. On you, more is still conservative. Relative to your size and colouring, more still looks like less. Even your hair can be a bit long, but must be styled and controlled, definitely in touch with the latest fashion.

■ Business clothes

You can easily achieve the businessman image. For business or dress you look best in a boldly structured silhouette, an average width lapel, vertical seams in the jacket and a slightly fitted waist. You may wear a single or double vent, depending on your personality and job environment. Your style calls for trousers without turn-ups unless your legs are so long that you want to minimise them. For social occasions you may want to buy a double-breasted suit. If your work allows you the freedom to be a little more stylish, do so. On you, less conservative clothes still *look* conservative because they are in harmony with your body type.

Dramatic

COLOUR FOR MEN

You look best in a dark, solid suit in navy, charcoal grey or brown, depending on your season, worn with crisp white or light shirts. You are also the perfect candidate for pinstriped suits. High-contrast prints – such as a light pinstripe on a dark background – are appropriately sharp on you, but you find most checks too blended or casual. A bold check in dark colours and a rough fabric could work for you. You don't wear tweeds well because they offer so little contrast, though a striking herringbone may be all right for variety.

You wear stiffer fabrics, such as heavy gabardine or smooth worsteds, with a firm finish and a crisp silhouette. No flannels for you – at least not the kind that look fuzzy. You're a formal fellow, really, and not very soft around the edges.

■ Dressy leisure wear

You dress boldly and favour extremes – either solid, dark-coloured blazers (maybe even double-breasted) or a heavily textured or patterned jacket (say a bold houndstooth check). Subtle tweeds just fade away on you. Pleated wool trousers are great, though you can wear non-pleated slacks just as well. You will always wear wool or cotton trousers rather than cords or jeans with your jacket.

■ Shirts

You look best in a crisp, light shirt (solid white, light pastel or icy) with a plain pointed collar, either regular or wide spread. Choose cotton with a hard finish for the sharpest look. Also excellent on you are bold stripes, hairline stripes and bold checks or plaids. A coloured shirt with a contrasting white collar and cuff might work – probably with a stripe, and usually best for Winters. You practically never wear cloth button-downs, knits, or checks or muted plaids. You tend to dress up a little more than the next fellow.

■ Ties

Your ties must always make a strong statement and offer sharp contrast to your shirts, though you can also wear a monochromatic look with a shirt and tie from the same colour family. Solid colours, especially dark or bright reds, are excellent. Your best patterns are stripes with bold contrasts, either a widely spaced pinstripe or widish stripes irregularly spaced. An overall geometric pattern is good. A small patterned tie is usually not expressive enough for you, but it may work if you choose one with a repeat pattern of high contrast and sharp lines (diamonds rather than circles). Any dot pattern should be extreme, preferably with large dots – medium looks boring on you. Any pattern you choose should offer contrast within the tie. Plaids and checks are too casual for you and club ties are too conservative. You look great in a silk tie with a sheen. One word of caution: be careful not to ruin your look with loud ties. A dramatic look simply calls for more contrast, darker or brighter colours, straight rather than curved lines and patterns.

■ Shoes

For work, your shoes are smooth and highly polished with a medium to thin sole and a slightly pointed toe. These shoes are okay for dressy leisure wear, too, though you may want a dressy pull-on shoe.

■ Casual wear

The Dramatic man always likes to make a fashion statement and dresses in outfits. For horseback riding you have riding clothes; for the tennis court, whites. Your casual clothes can be stripes or solids, again offering contrast, or brightly coloured cotton knit shirts. You are a man of extremes in texture and expression. If you are conservative, keep your casual clothes relatively formal with non-pleated slacks in wools (for cold weather) or cottons and gabardines. Jeans are your least good look because they are so average. Wear designer jeans, tight jeans or baggy jeans. Choose sweaters of heavy cable knits or geometric pattern or stripes, either form-fitting or on the baggy side. If a pair of silk lounging pyjamas and a smoking jacket really appeal to you, you know you have a Dramatic flair.

■ Coats

Your coat may be either a dark double-breasted overcoat of cashmere or fine wool or a heavily textured wraparound with a tie belt. Your trenchcoat can't be ordinary; go for something with a bold silhouette. Think oversize for coats. Wear anything big and bulky – you can carry it off! An extremely padded shoulder or a dropped shoulder makes a strong fashion statement for you, and dark colours work well.

■ Jewellery

Any jewellery you wear should look important. Your watch should be large rather than slimline, with either a textured leather or a metal band. You may wear a ring with a stone or large cufflinks that make a statement.

■ Formal

A dinner suit looks great on you. If you are a Winter, you'll stick to a black one because it looks so dashing on you.

Dramatic Prototypes
Sean Connery, Jeremy Irons, Clark Gable, Burt Lancaster, Charlton Heston

Romantic

You are the man who calls for a *rich, luxurious, well-blended* look. The Romantic is a Romeo – a lover, not a fighter. You're gracious and suave, with the air of an artist or poet about you. Very sensual and very social, you have expensive tastes and a bit of theatrical flair. Everything about you suggests wealth, sophistication and the bedroom. The Romantic is a 'people' person and can be found in highly visible positions, both at work and at play. In general, you're naturally interested in fashion and grooming, and you need to restrain your flamboyance rather than strive for an energetic look.

The Romantic man is moderately tall with an athletic but not overdeveloped build – strong but not bulky. Romantics tend to have beautiful eyes and skin and thick hair – curly, wavy or straight, but always luxuriant. Your face is expressive and well-proportioned, important to your overall look. Sophisticated and sexy, you're influenced by current fashions and have a love of soft fabrics and luxurious colours. A rather formal dresser, you choose clothes fitted to show off your body symmetry; all detail serves to frame your face.

■ Business clothes

If you work in a field that allows for less conservative dress, you can really go for a high-fashion look. A fitted suit is your best look, with either double vents or no vent (a single vent is too boxy for you). Padded shoulders and a very nipped-in waist flatter your lithe silhouette. A double-breasted jacket is good for you, too. If your profession requires a conservative image, choose the suit with a definite waist and padded shoulder. Avoid sharp lines in favour of a smooth, slightly curved silhouette. Choose fine wools and cashmere rather than stiff fabrics or gabardine. Soft, lightweight woollens suit your look and your expensive tastes. Your favourite textured fabric is very soft: your favourite colours are the richest (not darkest) of your palette – lush colours of medium intensity such as rich navy or warm coffee brown. For suits, solids are best, though stripes in soft textures and woven-in designs can work well for you. Patterns, if any, should be on a small scale, and checks or plaids aren't really for you.

■ Dressy leisure wear

This is your best style – the clothes in which you are most comfortable. The Romantic favours elegant leisure wear – a fitted cashmere jacket, for example. He avoids patterned jackets or any highly contrasting separates. He wears trendy looks. Pleated trousers are fine as long as they are fairly fitted in the hips and buttocks. You enjoy special jackets, such as one that's short and fitted in a buttery

Romantic

leather, or something long and draped and stylish. Soft wool, suede, and silk make excellent jackets for you.

■ Shirts

Since your face is one of your best features, unusual collars are your forte. Collar pins or lapel pins are excellent on you, as are wing collars or any very high collars. For business attire, wear an unstarched standard collar in a thin, smooth cotton, and in other professions choose a fabric such as silk or cotton batiste. Avoid overly crisp shirts – they are cold for a Romantic. Do wear some colour, rather than white, but stick mostly to solids. Stripes are not your best look unless they are very well-blended and soft.

■ Ties

Go for silk, either shiny or raw (matt), in a well-blended design – never a knit or woven tie. Solids are your absolute best. Since your overall look is harmonious, choose a tie that is in medium contrast to your shirt, either solids or a pattern that has colours from both your jacket and shirt. In patterns, stripes must be well-blended and paisleys are best in shiny silk with a watercolour effect. Small patterned ties are not the Romantic's best look because they are too crisp and predictable. If you need them for business wear, choose repeat patterns in teardrop or oval shapes. Pin dots on shiny silk are good, but avoid medium or large dots. Avoid patterns with rigid structures or defined edges. Unusual ties – narrow ones, for example – are good.

■ Shoes

Choose a lightweight Italian-look shoe with a thin sole, or an elegant boot of very fine, soft leather or suede.

■ Casual wear

Both elegant and trendy, your casual wear should look expensive and reflect your sophisticated flamboyance. You wear designer jeans, smooth leather trousers and fashion colours. Choose a short leather jacket with epaulettes or a military jacket with lots of detail.

■ Coats

Overcoats must have shape and a fitted silhouette. Padded shoulders are important and wrap belts work well. Choose soft woollens or cashmere if possible.

■ Jewellery

Used as an accent and not overdone, jewellery is great on the Romantic man – a ring with a stone, for example, but no heavy neck chains. Your watch is a simple but elegant slimline with either a metal or smooth leather band. Think tasteful and subtle.

YOUR CLOTHING PERSONALITY

■ Formal

A truly formal look, though flattering, can look too severe on you. Although a fussy look doesn't suit you, you can take some liberties with your formal look – a jewelled lapel pin, a white dinner jacket or a red tie. Tails and a fitted waist in your formal jacket work for you. If the occasion allows, try something different, such as a velvet jacket and silk shirt over designer jeans.

Romantic Prototypes
Richard Gere, Michael Jackson, Omar Sharif, Michael York, Dudley Moore

Natural

You are the man who calls for textures, tweeds, informality and a *blended* look.

The Natural man is usually of sturdy or athletic build. Your face may be craggy with irregular features, or perhaps you have a square jaw and wide-set eyes or simply a rugged and outdoorsy look. You might have freckles, and your hair is rarely glossy. Your stride is easy and you have a down-to-earth look about you. The Natural is an informal dresser who is rarely comfortable all dressed up and gets the most compliments in jeans and sweaters. You look best in casual, relaxed clothing and in the colours from your palette that are closest to nature, especially the browns, greens and blues. Your hair is loose and wavy, or short, straight and layered – casual rather than overly controlled, and always with the dry look. You're the man who can wear a beard or moustache well.

■ Business clothes

A two-piece suit is better for you than a three-piece, which looks overly formal and stuffy on you. Your suit should be fuller cut, with a relaxed shoulder. If you are athletic but thin, you will have to buy a slimmer cut suit, but it should not be tapered too much at the waist. You would never wear trendy cuts in suits.

Your best suits for work are solid flannels in a medium colour, or perhaps a subtle check, tweed, or other pattern. Dark solids may look severe on you, and pinstripes are definitely too formal and stiff. (You *can* survive in the business world without owning a pinstripe!) At most you would wear a subtle chalk stripe, preferably in colours without much contrast.

Your best fabrics are heavyish with some texture and always a matt (non-shiny) finish or a nap: flannel, corduroy, and looser weaves. Nothing shiny, fancy or too formal.

Natural

■ **Dressy leisure wear**

If your work environment allows for slacks and jackets, so much the better. You are better looking in a jacket than in a suit. Think texture. A corduroy jacket or a heavy wool, tweed or check are your best looks. A camel jacket is ideal for you if you are an Autumn or Spring. Your best dress-up attire is leisure wear whenever possible, and you can be quite natty in a country tweed with leather patches on the elbows, and perhaps a polo neck instead of a shirt and tie. Patch pockets and topstitching really are your look.

■ **Shirts**

You are best in cotton for work and for social occasions except when the event calls for formal attire. Button-down collars are great for you. Checks and plaids are your best patterns. Subtle, blended, broad stripes are all right, but no severe or formal hairline stripes.

■ **Ties**

You go for less sharp contrast in your coat, shirt and tie combinations. The mono-chromatic look – using colours from the same family in varying degrees of intensity – is ideal for the Natural. Your best tie patterns are tartans or plaids and checks or wide stripes in muted colours, creating a blended look. Ties with square designs are better than rounds or ovals. No dots for you – they're too formal. Paisleys are sophisticated yet natural, especially in the warm palettes, and are a good dress look for the Natural man. Texture and matt finishes are also good. Ribbed knits, woods, rough-weave linen (in summer), and non-shiny silks are best.

■ **Shoes**

Shoes for the Natural are dressy pull-ons for business and more casual ones for leisure wear. You may wear a textured leather shoe with a heavy sole and topstitching, with your tweed jacket. Your shoes have a widish toe rather than a pointed or very rounded one.

■ **Casual wear**

Casual wear is your thing. You may prefer to wear the colours closest to nature in your palette, and you definitely wear natural fabrics such as linen looks and cotton. Wear khakis, cords, and jeans with turtlenecks, check flannel shirts, button-downs or short-sleeved cottons and T-shirts for warm weather. As usual for you, plaids, checks and solids in rough fabrics are best. Your sweaters are crewnecks or bulky, textured pullovers. No Fair Isle or fancy patterns. Non-shiny leather is best for boots, belts or any accessories.

■ **Coats**

You may not want a coat because they are so formal, and you can wear your trenchcoat almost anywhere now, anyway. If you do want a wool topcoat, choose a double- or single-breasted camel coat if you're a warm season, or a single-breasted beige or blue if you're a cool season. Shaggy furs suit you well, as do non-shiny leathers such as sheepskin. Your trenchcoat is either the single-breasted simple one with raglan sleeves or a traditional military trench with epaulettes and heavy trim. If you are a thin and lanky Natural, forget the trimmings; they'll over-whelm you.

■ Jewellery

If any, it would be heavy and masculine – but probably you don't wear any. Your watch should not be too thin, and could have a leather strap rather than a metal band.

■ Formal

A dinner suit is your least favourite item of clothing. Choose a simple pleated shirt in the colour of your season. For other social occasions, the Natural man can always dress in sportier attire than the Dramatic or Classic man. On you, a beaut-iful jacket, wool slacks, a shirt, and a tie look dressy. For weddings, funerals, and formal affairs, wear your suit in a medium colour rather than a dark one.

Natural Prototypes
Alan Alda, Harrison Ford, Robert Redford, Clint Eastwood, Michael Caine, Ian Botham, Alan Bates

Classic

The Classic man's looks call for *simplicity*, *quality* and *moderation*.

Your body is of average proportions, not too tall or short, neither lanky nor extremely muscular. Your facial features are evenly proportioned and regular with no prominent features such as big nose or a very square jaw. Your face has refined features and your colouring is medium. Everything about you is sophisticated and moderate. Your demeanour is conservative, poised, slightly formal but not stuffy. Nothing you wear should be extreme in style, fabric, texture, or colour. Simplicity of line and detail suit you best. You are the traditional type, a fashion conservative. Because you do not look good in fads, gimmicks, or high-fashion clothes, or in any form of bold or extreme patterns, you must rely on fine fabric and beautifully tailored, conservative clothes. You cannot get away with rumpled or ill-fitting clothing. You must look fastidious, even if it's not truly your nature. You look best with a relatively short, conservative hairstyle – always combed and neatly in place.

Classic

■ Business clothes

For business you wear two-piece suits on most days, reserving three-piece suits for important meetings or dressy occasions. You wear a traditional suit. Choose one with a relaxed, unstructured shoulder but slightly trimmer at the waist. You don't want topstitching or any sporty or faddish details.

Because Classic represents the middle value in body type, size, and colouring, you look great in most classic patterns as long as they are moderate in scale and contrast – a subdued pinstripe or chalk stripe, for example, or a small check or medium-scaled, subtle plaid. Your season dictates your best patterns: Winters in stripes and herringbones; Summers in stripes and soft tweeds; Autumns in tweeds and small checks or plaids; Springs in plaids and checks. Solids are excellent for all.

Your best fabrics are light- to medium-weight worsteds or very thin, tightly woven flannels and tweeds with a firm finish.

■ Dressy sportswear

Your first jacket is a solid single-breasted blazer in a nice wool fabric. Next is a herringbone or tweed in a fairly fine texture. You do not wear heavily textured or boldly patterned fabrics well, even in leisure wear. Classic styles in wool slacks are for you – no exaggerated pleats, flared legs or trendy items. You may wear tweed or checked wool slacks for a bit of dash.

■ Shirts

You go for an understated look, and are best in white or solid pastel shirts (especially blue) in button-down for day and plain collars for evening or special occasions. For a natty look, you may wear a coloured shirt with a white collar. You don't wear many patterned shirts, save an occasional subtle stripe or a white on white. Although plaids and checks are not your thing, you can wear a small check with a solid blazer for sport. In general, you'll wear a shirt and tie rather than a turtleneck with your jacket for special events.

■ Ties

Your tie is also conservative, but it does not have to be dull. Small patterned ties are your best pattern, with the repeats in oval or rounded shapes. You can wear thin, evenly spaced stripes, or irregular stripes in moderate widths and traditional colours. Club ties are great, especially with a jacket, but most checks or plaids are too casual and sporty for you. A silk tie is your best fabric, though thin wools and linens (in summer) are fine, too. Either a matt or a slight sheen works well on you. A slight sheen is best as a dressy look. Never wear any loud or boldly patterned tie; there is nothing eccentric about your body, so you can't wear eccentric clothing.

■ Shoes

Shoes for business are lace-ups with a medium sole and wide-cut toe. The leather can be smooth or lightly textured. If you're the elegant type, you may wear a smooth lace-up with a rounded toe, especially for dress. For sportswear you wear your lace-ups or a dressy slip-on shoe.

■ Casual wear

The Classic man's casual clothes are crisp and clean. Wool or cotton trousers, ironed blue jeans (if any) with cloth button-downs in the winter and knit shirts in the summer. Although you will probably not wear way-out colours in sports shirts, you can wear fun colours in basic reds, blues, greens, and yellows.

■ Coats

Your best topcoat is a single-breasted wool with simple details – no topstitching, epaulettes, etc. Your trenchcoat may be single- or double-breasted, but again with simple styling and no gimmicks. The traditional coat is your look as well.

■ Jewellery

Jewellery for the Classic is tasteful, refined, and minimal. A thin watch with a metal or smooth leather band works well for you. A ring is all right, but no bracelets or neck chains.

■ Formal

You look great in a dinner jacket because it gives you the opportunity to dress like a Dramatic but within the confines of tradition. You look better in average lapels rather than those pointing upwards towards the shoulder. Choose pleated shirts rather than ruffles. You also look great dressed up in a three-piece suit, which adds variety to your usual two-piece or business look.

Classic Prototypes
Cary Grant, Gregory Peck, Anthony Perkins, Roger Moore, Laurence Olivier

YOUR OWN BEST LOOK

Many men can look believable in more than one look. Paul Newman's image in a fisherman's knit sweater is just as credible as his lawyer image in a three-piece suit. Warren Beatty can smooth his hair into a conservative, traditional style and go to work at IBM, wear his hair wavy and loose and hang out in cords and sweaters, *or* dress in structured suits and look dramatic. His looks are so versatile that simply by changing his hair and his demeanour he can pull off almost any clothing image.

Whatever image you favour, just be sure it's believable on you. You have undoubtedly seen someone whose clothing was socially acceptable but looked all wrong on *him*. Give yourself permission not to buy a tweed jacket for variety if you are a formal Winter who will always look best in a solid blazer. Skip the pinstripe if you're a rugged outdoorsman caught in the trappings of a business environment. No one will ever notice that you don't own a pinstripe. They'll just know that you always look nice in what you *do* have.

Understanding your clothing personality takes time and some experimenting. The basic thing to remember is that what feels right and looks good is probably right.

Dramatic Type

BUSINESS	CASUAL
Suits	**Jackets**
Square shoulders	Square shoulders
Nipped-in waist	Single- or double-breasted
Single, double or no vent	May be unconstructed
Two- or three-piece	Smooth or very rough
Peaked or notched lapels	Wool, cotton, silk, blends
Worsted wools	Solids
Gabardine	Heavy tweeds
Silk blends	Houndstooth
Solids	
Bold herringbone	**Trousers**
Large box check	Wool, cotton, firm weave
Bold plaid (design, not colour)	Plain or pleated
Pinstripe – narrow or wider	Plain or with turn-ups
	Straight or tapered
Shirts	**Shirts**
Cotton or cotton-polyester	Cotton or cotton-polyester
Solids	Solids
Thin stripe (crisp)	Bold check or plaid
Wide stripe	Bold stripes
Plain or spread collar	
Ties	**Leisure Wear**
Silk – sheen	Costumes (outfits that fit activity)
Dark solids	Bulky knit sweaters
Large-scale patterns	Lounging attire
Stripes – sharp contrast	Cotton knit shirts – bright
Overall geometrics	Stripes, geometric patterns
Small patterned (high contrast)	
Accessories	
Cufflinks	
Large watch	
Braces	

Romantic Type

BUSINESS	CASUAL

BUSINESS

Suits
Padded shoulders
Pinched-in waist
Double or no vent
Single- or double-breasted
Two-piece
Soft wools, silks, blends
Solids
Subtle stripes
Woven-in designs

Shirts
Cotton or cotton/polyester, silk, batiste
Solids
Stripe – subtle, blended
Plain collars

Ties
Silk – sheen
Medium-colour solids
Medium-scale patterns
Stripes – wide, blended
Small patterned – rounded patterns
Paisley

Accessories
Stickpin
Rings
Thin chains
Slimline watch

CASUAL

Jackets
Square or natural shoulders
May be unconstructed
Single- or double-breasted
Smooth textures
Wool, silk, blends, leather
Solids

Trousers
Corduroy, leather
Pleated or plain
No turn-ups
Tapered

Shirts
Silk, batiste
Solids
Unusual collars

Leisure Wear
Italian styling
Short, fitted jackets
Soft sweaters

Natural Type

BUSINESS	CASUAL

Suits

Natural shoulders
Full-cut
Slightly pinched-in waist (if thin)
Single vent
Single-breasted
Two-piece
Flannel, cotton, linen
Tweed
Herringbone
Large box check
Subtle chalk stripe
Plaid or small check

Jackets

Natural shoulders
Single breasted
Rough textures
Wool, cotton, linen, blends, corduroy
Heavy tweed
Houndstooth
Plaid
Elbow patches
Patch pockets
Topstitching

Shirts

Cotton or cotton-polyester
Stripes – wide, subtle
Checks
Button-down

Trousers

Wool, cotton, corduroy, denim
Plain or pleated
Plain or with turn-ups
Straight or tapered

Ties

Silk – matt
Ribbed knit
Heavy wool
Linen
Medium-colour solids
Medium-scale patterns
Stripes – wide, blended
Small patterned – square designs
Club
Paisley
Plaid

Shirts

Cotton or cotton/polyester
Stripes – wide
Plaid
Checks

Leisure Wear

Turtlenecks
Bulky sweaters
Boots
Athletic outfits

Accessories

Watch with leather band

Classic Type

BUSINESS

Suits
Slightly padded shoulders
Slightly nipped-in waist or full cut
Single or double vent
Single-breasted
Two- or three-piece
Worsted, flannel, cotton, blends
Tweed
Herringbone
Small box check
Pinstripe – narrow
Chalk stripe

Shirts
Cotton or cotton/polyester
Solids
Subtle stripes
Button-down or plain collar

Ties
Silk – sheen, matt
Wool – smooth
Linen
Medium to dark solids
Medium-scale patterns
Stripes – thin, even or medium, uneven
Small patterned – rounded, geometric
Club

Accessories
Watch – metal or leather band

CASUAL

Jackets
Slightly padded to natural shoulder
Single- or double-breasted
Smooth textures
Solids
Subtle tweed, plaid
Houndstooth

Trousers
Wool, cotton, corduroy (stiff)
Plain or with turn-ups
Straight legs

Shirts
Blends
Solids
Button-down

Leisure Wear
Cotton knit shirts
Trousers with small checks
Nautical motifs

CHAPTER THIRTEEN

SHOPPING

Most men dislike shopping for two reasons: they resent the time involved and they feel unsure of their choices. The Colour for Men system will cut your shopping time to a minimum. And you will not waste any money on a mistake. If you have been depending on someone else to select your clothes or have simply been buying the same items year in and year out, now's the time for you to discover how to enjoy speedy, successful shopping.

Here are some tips to help make shopping efficient and rewarding.

Shop with your colours and look only at items in your colours
Always shop with your colour chart. Your eye cannot retain the memory of a colour for more than a few seconds. You may think you have spotted your red tie, only to find when you get home that it's the wrong red. Hold your chart against the garment in question. If it blends, it's yours. If it clashes, put it back.

Your palette works as a general guide, but be particularly careful when choosing colours that are difficult for you to wear. Winters should match their taupe (grey beige) and lemon yellow closely. Summers should match their light lemon yellow and rose beige as closely as possible, too. Autumns must take care with their marine navy and periwinkle, and Springs should match their greys and navies closely. Here *fabric swatches* will be your best guide, as it is difficult to reproduce colours in print with extreme accuracy.

Shop lights often distort colours, so look at the item under natural light if possible.

When buying a patterned garment – check, plaid or tweed, for example – make sure the fabric falls within your palette by comparing its overall background colour to your *solid-colour swatch*. The effect should be the same in both.

It's all right if some of the pattern includes bits of colours that are not yours. The rule of thumb is not to let that 'off' colour ruin your total look. Bear the following in mind.

■ Don't allow the wrong colour to dominate.
■ Don't allow the wrong colour to force you to buy a tie, belt or shoes in the wrong colour.
■ Don't wear the wrong colour near your face.

For example, a thread that is not your colour may be woven through the background of a suit. That's fine as long as you don't buy a tie in that colour. (It will often limit your tie selection.) Or you may find a pair of plaid slacks that contains colours from more than one season. Fine, as long as you can pull *your* colour out for your shirt.

Say 'no' to clothes that aren't in your colours
Learn to say 'no' to items that are not in your colours. Discipline yourself not to even look at them. Decisions will then be easy, you'll save time, and you guarantee yourself a co-ordinated wardrobe with myriad clothing combinations. The minute you add one off-colour item, you complicate your wardrobe plan, and getting dressed will be so much harder.

Recognise when a bargain is not a bargain
By saying 'yes' only to sale items in your colours, you can be assured that everything you buy will go with whatever you own now or buy next year. Anything you buy on sale that doesn't look good on you is really a waste of money, not a saving.

Be aware of the clothing industry's colour cycles and be open-minded about which colour you want to buy
Don't shop with a preconceived idea of a colour you want to buy. Instead, be open-minded about what's available in your colours. The clothing industry does not promote every colour every year. With the exception of basic business colours – navy and grey – most colours come in cycles several years apart. If you are hankering to try out your emerald green cotton knit shirt but you don't see that particular shade of green in the stores, forget it for now. You'll just be wasting your time hunting for it. Choose something in vogue now, as long as it's your colour. Next year emerald green will probably be everywhere!

Your season will usually be your best shopping time of year. During your off-season you may have to search for some of your colours. Stock up during your best shopping season on shirts and even suits in your colours that you can wear year-round.

Find a salesperson who is your season
Any salesperson, male or female, automatically likes his or her own colours. Unless you are in a store where the personnel have been specifically trained to understand colour, the salesperson is likely to sell you his or her colours instead of yours. Even with your chart handy, he or she is likely to 'see' his or her blue instead of your blue. A salesperson who is your season will intuitively be of more help to you.

By the same token, shopping with a wife or friend who is not your season can produce the same unhappy results. Don't shop with a friend or spouse unless you're sure he/she understands your colours.

Find your shop
The buyer in a shop influences the selection of all the merchandise. If the buyer is your season, you're in luck. She/he will intuitively select not only lots of your colours but also styles, fabrics and patterns that suit you, too.

Furthermore, get to know which labels are cut and styled for you. Some stores will carry your cut; others won't.

Dress appropriately; be well groomed
If you are shopping for jeans, it's fine to wear jeans and sneakers to the store. If you want to buy a suit, wear a suit! Not only do you need the shirt and shoes for a proper fit, but it's also impossible to judge the look of even the finest suit when you're wearing a pair of old sneakers. Wear a solid tie and chances are it will go with the suit. You can assess an outfit more successfully if you look the part. Comb your hair and shave. You will command the attention of the store personnel and therefore receive better service. A scruffy customer hardly looks like a good bet to a top-notch salesperson.

Spend the most money on the clothes you wear the most
If you wear a suit once a year, buy an inexpensive suit. But a suit worn every day won't hold its shape or wear well unless the fabric and tailoring are both of good quality. In this case, it's a waste of money to buy an inexpensive suit.

COLOUR FOR MEN

Develop a shopping routine

First go to your size. If you're not sure of your size, have the salesperson measure you. Then pull out everything in your colours. Next choose the style and pattern. Check fabric and quality. Now try on.

This shopping routine helps you to quickly sort out the possibilities. If nothing passes the first few steps, go to another store. You've put in little effort and you still have the time, energy, and money to go elsewhere.

Once you buy a suit, have the salesperson give you a swatch of the material after the suit is fitted. Keep your swatches on a large safety pin and hang the pin on your tie rack. When you shop, you can take the swatches along to remind you of the suits you already have, as well as to help you pick out new shirts and ties.

Make a list

Using the Survival List, itemise the clothing you need to complete your wardrobe. If money is an issue, arrange the list in order of priority. Perhaps you need a coat and a suit, but both are expensive; decide which you need more and put it at the top of the list. Shopping with a list prevents hit-or-miss impulse purchases that eat up your budget and keep you from being able to buy that second item that you really need.

It's also a good idea to tack a piece of paper and a pen to your wardrobe door. When you notice you need some item of clothing, jot it down. When it's time to shop, your list is already compiled.

Go through your wardrobe

Go through your wardrobe and remove everything you haven't worn for a year. If you haven't worn it for a whole year, chances are you never will. Give those clothes away. Automatically you will be removing clothes that don't fit, that are out of style or that you simply don't like.

If your weight fluctuates, remove the wrong-size-for-now clothes and put them in a box or storage wardrobe for a later date. Keep in your wardrobe only the clothes you really wear. An organised wardrobe simplifies getting dressed and leads to an organised day.

To avoid all that wasted space at the bottom of your wardrobe, have a carpenter instal a second pole halfway between the floor and the standard pole. Hang your shirts and coats on the top pole, your trousers on the bottom. Put your dressing-gown on a hook. You may also want to build in racks or open drawers for your shoes or folded shirts and sweaters.

Shop twice a year

The clothing industry promotes warm weather clothes at the end of winter and cool weather clothes in summer. If you want to buy summer clothes in the summer, forget it. There's nothing left. At the end of winter, buy everything you need for spring and summer. In summer, buy all your autumn and winter clothes. During these seasons the selection is good and you can purchase everything on your list in four hours or less, including trips to different shops for shoes or whatever. Add a couple of hours for return trips for fittings and you have shopping down to ten hours or less per year.

By buying ahead of need you will never have to give up your Saturday golf or tennis because you were invited to a party on Saturday night.

WHEN SOMEONE SHOPS FOR YOU...

If you really hate to shop, you can give your favourite salesperson the Survival List and your colour chart. If you are colour-blind, you will have to let someone help you find your colours.

Shopping may never be your favourite pastime, but your colours certainly make it easier and less time-consuming. I know some men who have become shopping converts now that the frustration has been removed. Also, many men have had the selection of their clothes controlled by other people since their early childhood years. You may now enjoy having the freedom to shop for yourself, buying clothes that you like and knowing that you will look better than ever!

SHOPPING GUIDE FOR A WINTER MAN

Neutrals	Lights	Basic Colours	Brights/Accents
Navy	Pure White	True Blue	Royal Blue
Black	Icy Grey	Pine Green	Hot Turquoise
Taupe (Grey Beige)	Icy Blue	Bright Burgundy	Chinese Blue
Charcoal Grey	Icy Yellow	Blue Red	Lemon Yellow
Medium True Grey	Icy Pink		Light True Green
Light True Grey	Icy Green		True Green
	Icy Violet		Emerald Green
	Icy Aqua		True Red
			Shocking Pink
			Deep Hot Pink
			Magenta
			Fuchsia
			Royal Purple

Suits, Trousers

Select suits and trousers from your neutral group. Neutrals form the foundation of your wardrobe because they go with everything.

Patterns: Winters are best in solids or pinstripes that offer sharp contrasts.

Business/Dress Shirts

Choose business and dress shirts from the Lights category. Wear them as solids or with stripes or checks from any of your colour groups (e.g., White shirt with Bright Burgundy stripe). Shirt colours are important, since they are worn next to the face.

Casual Clothes

Casual clothes may be worn in Brights/Accents as solids or in stripes or other prints, according to your personality. Here's your chance to add a new dimension to your casual wardrobe.

Jackets

Select from the Basic colour or Neutral groups. Basic colours are versatile, go with many of your other colours and add interest to your wardrobe.

Ties

Ties can bring life to your overall appearance. Select colours from any group that relate to your shirt and jacket – Neutrals or Basic colours for a more conservative look. Winters are best in solids or contrasting stripes, but can also wear polka dots or small patterns that contain some sharpness.

Shoes and Belts
Black, Navy, Brownish and Grey are the appropriate colours here. For warm weather, add Taupe or White.

Overcoat
Choose Black, Navy, Grey, or Taupe (Grey Beige), whichever is your best.

Shopping Reminder
(List Sizes)

Shirt: Neck _____   Sleeve _____

Sports shirt _____

Suit/Jacket _____

Waist _____

Trouser length _____

Sock _____

Shoe _____

Glove _____

Overcoat _____

Other _____

_____

SHOPPING GUIDE FOR A SUMMER MAN

Neutrals	Lights	Basic Colours	Brights/Accents
Greyish Navy	Soft White	Cadet Blue	Light Lemon Yellow
Charcoal Blue Grey	Light Rose Beige	Burgundy	Sky Blue
Light Blue Grey	Powder Blue	Blue Red	Medium Blue
Greyish Blue	Light Periwinkle	Spruce Green	Periwinkle Blue
Rose Brown	Blue		Pastel Aqua
Cocoa	Pale Lemon Yellow		Pastel Blue Green
Rose Beige	Powder Pink		Medium Blue Green
	Light Mauve		Deep Blue Green
	Lavender		Watermelon Red
			Pastel Pink
			Rose Pink
			Deep Rose
			Orchid
			Mauve
			Raspberry
			Soft Fuchsia
			Plum

Suits, Trousers

Select suits and trousers from your Neutral group. Neutrals form the foundation of your wardrobe because they go with everything.

Patterns: Summers are best in solids or subtle patterns that offer minimal contrast.

Business/Dress Shirts

Choose business and dress shirts from the Lights category. Wear them as solids, or with stripes or checks from any of your colour groups (e.g., Soft White shirt with Blue stripe). Shirt colours are important, since they are worn next to the face.

Casual Clothes

Casual clothes may be worn in Brights/Accents as solids or in stripes or other prints, according to your personality. Here's your chance to add a new dimension to your casual wardrobe.

Jackets

Select from the Basic colour or Neutral groups. Basic colours are versatile, go with many of your other colours and add interest to your wardrobe.

Ties

Ties can bring life to your overall appearance. Select colours from any group that relate to your shirt and jacket – Neutrals or Basic colours for a more conservative look. Summers are best in subtle patterns – small dots or patterns or blended stripes.

Shoes and Belts

Rose Brown, Black, Navy, Brownish and Grey are the appropriate colours here. For warm weather, add Rose Beige or Soft White.

Overcoat

Choose Navy, Greyish Blue, Rose Brown or Cocoa, whichever is your best.

Shopping Reminder

(List Sizes)

Shirt: Neck _____ Sleeve _____

Sports shirt _____

Suit/Jacket _____

Waist _____

Trouser length _____

Sock _____

Shoe _____

Glove _____

Overcoat _____

Other _____

_____

SHOPPING GUIDE FOR A AUTUMN MAN

Neutrals	Lights	Basic Colours	Brights/Accents
Charcoal Brown	Oyster White	Forest Green	Yellow Gold
Dark Chocolate Brown	Warm Beige	Medium Warm Bronze	Mustard
Coffee Brown	Light Gold	Rust	Pumpkin
Khaki/Tan	Light Peach/ Apricot	Mahogany	Terracotta
Camel	Light Periwinkle Blue	Gold	Deep Peach/ Apricot
Marine Navy	Light Greyish Green	Teal Blue	Salmon
Olive Green			Orange
Greyish Green			Orange Red
			Bittersweet Red
			Dark Tomato Red
			Jade Green
			Lime Green
			Moss Green
			Bright Yellow Green
			Turquoise
			Deep Periwinkle Blue

Suits, Trousers

Select suits and trousers from your Neutral group. Neutrals form the foundation of your wardrobe because they go with everything.

Patterns: Autumns are often best in tweeds, plaids and rich, rough fabrics.

Business/Dress Shirts

Choose business and dress shirts from the Lights category. Wear them as solids or with stripes or checks from any of your colour groups (e.g., Oyster White shirt with Rust stripe). Shirt colours are important, since they are worn next to the face.

Casual Clothes

Casual clothes may be worn in Brights/Accents as solids or in stripes or other prints, according to your personality. Here's your chance to add a new dimension to your casual wardrobe.

Jackets

Select jackets from the Basic colour or Neutral groups. Basic colours are versatile, go with many of your other colours and add interest to your wardrobe.

Ties
Ties can bring life to your overall appearance. Select colours from any group that relate to your shirt and jacket – Neutrals or Basic colours for a more conservative look. Autumns are best with rich colours worn in paisleys, tartans, plaids, irregular stripes or small patterns.

Shoes and Belts
Brown, Brownish Burgundy Black (with navy), and Tan are the appropriate colours here. For warm weather, add Beige or Oyster.

Overcoat
Choose Charcoal Brown, Coffee, Khaki/Tan, Camel or Marine Navy, whichever is your best.

Shopping Reminder
(List Sizes)

Shirt: Neck _____   Sleeve _____

Sports shirt _____

Suit/Jacket _____

Waist _____

Trouser length _____

Sock _____

Shoe _____

Glove _____

Overcoat _____

Other _____

_____

SHOPPING GUIDE FOR A SPRING MAN

Neutrals	Lights	Basic Colours	Brights/Accents
Clear Bright Navy	Ivory	Light Clear Navy	Pastel Yellow Green
Medium Warm Grey	Buff	Light Clear Gold	Bright Yellow Green
Light Warm Grey	Light Peach/	Light Rust	Light Warm Aqua
Chocolate Brown	Apricot	Light Teal Blue	Clear Bright Aqua
Medium Golden	Warm Pastel Pink		Emerald Turquoise
Brown	Light Clear Blue		Light True Blue
Golden Tan	Light Periwinkle		Periwinkle Blue
Camel	Blue		Dark Periwinkle
Light Warm Beige			Blue
			Medium Violet
			Bright Golden
			Yellow
			Peach/Apricot
			Clear Salmon
			Clear Bright Warm
			Pink
			Coral Pink
			Bright Coral
			Light Orange
			Orange Red
			Clear Bright Red

Suits, Trousers

Select suits and trousers from your Neutral group. Neutrals form the foundation of your wardrobe because they go with everything.

Patterns: Springs are often best in checks, plaids or solids with a slight texture.

Business/Dress Shirts

Choose business and dress shirts from the Lights category. Wear them as solids or with stripes or checks from any of your colour groups (e.g., Ivory shirt with Blue stripe). Shirt colours are important, since they are worn next to the face.

Casual Clothes

Casual clothes may be worn in Brights/Accents as solids or in stripes or other prints, according to your personality. Here's your chance to add a new dimension to your casual wardrobe.

Jackets

Select from the Basic colour or Neutral groups. Basic colours are versatile, go with many of your other colours and add interest to your wardrobe.

Ties

Ties can bring life to your overall appearance. Select colours from any group that relate to your shirt and jacket – Neutrals or Basic colours for a more conservative look. Springs are best in solids or subtle prints: plaids, stripes, small patterns.

Shoes and Belts

Brown, Tan, Brownish Burgundy and Black (with navy) are the appropriate colours here. For warm weather, add Beige and Ivory.

Overcoat

Choose Camel, Medium Warm Grey, Golden Tan or Light Clear Navy, whichever is your best.

Shopping Reminder
(List Sizes)

Shirt: Neck _____ Sleeve _____

Sports shirt _____

Suit/Jacket _____

Waist _____

Trouser length _____

Sock _____

Shoe _____

Glove _____

Overcoat _____

Other _____

_____

CHAPTER FOURTEEN

THE FINISHING TOUCHES: HAIR, GLASSES AND GROOMING

HAIRSTYLE AND FACE SHAPE

No programme to improve your looks is complete without attention to your hair. We've all seen the man who is well dressed and yet still doesn't look pulled together. A shaggy haircut or an unkempt beard can ruin the effect. Not only does a flattering haircut strengthen your best facial features and hide your flaws, but it also enhances your overall image. A poor haircut does the opposite.

Finding the best hairstyle is harder for a man than for a woman. While women have flexibility, men can make only subtle adjustments in their hairstyle. In most businesses, hair must be relatively short; even so, the variation of a centimetre in length can transform your face. The placement of your parting, the length of the hair around your ears, a layered or blunt cut – all make a significant difference in your look.

Your best hairstyle depends on your face shape, the type of hair (curly, straight, thin, thick), your lifestyle and the amount of time and care you are willing to devote to your hair. To decide how to get the cut that is best for you, let's see what face shape you have and how to work with it. There are seven basic shapes: oval, diamond, round, square, rectangle, oblong, and triangle. Pull your hair back from your face, look in the mirror and examine the outline. Then choose from the following the category that most closely fits your face. You probably won't fit into an exact category, but having a sense of your general face shape will help you decide on a good haircut.

Oval

This is the 'perfect' face shape. Slightly wider at the forehead than at the cheek-bones or chin, it is classically proportioned.

If you have an oval face, you can wear any hairstyle that suits your personality and lifestyle. Don't be afraid to change and experiment with new looks, for you can carry them off.

Round

A round face is also wider at the cheekbones but has a curved chin and brow. It is almost as wide as it is long.

Your goal is to slim your face and create a longer look. Your hair can also help create the illusion of angles. Part your hair about five centimetres or two inches to either side of centre with a fringe on an angle to cut the roundness of your forehead. Keep fullness at the top and around eye level, but trim hair shorter at the ears. Wear your sideburns a touch longer and cut them on an angle with the front pointing downward. A closely trimmed beard shaped at an angle can effectively slim a round face.

Square

A square face is about as wide at the cheeks as it as long, with an angular jaw and a square forehead.

If your face is square, your goal is to make your face seem a little longer and somewhat less angular. Keep your parting six or seven centimetres (about 1½ in) to either side of centre, as a part too far to the side accents squareness. Hair should be full on top, adding height. Cover the corners of your angular forehead so that your hair waves outward at both temples.

Rectangle

Longer than it is wide, the rectangular face is square-jawed and has an angular forehead.

If your face is rectangular, you can shorten it slightly by adding fullness to the sides and softening the hairline. Cover your forehead with an off-centre fringe to shorten your face and camouflage your angular forehead. A layered cut adds width and helps create roundness at the sides of your face. Blow-dry your hair to add fullness. Avoid long hair at the back.

Triangle

A wide brow, slightly narrower cheekbones and a narrow chin are characteristic of the triangular face.

Oval

Round

Square

Rectangle

If your face is triangular, you need to narrow your brow area and widen your chin. Part your hair about eight centimetres or three inches to either side of centre with a fringe covering one side of the forehead. Keep it close-cropped at the top and temples, with extra length and fullness at the back, perhaps showing beneath the ears. A beard can be the perfect solution for filling in a narrow chin.

Triangle

GLASSES

The correct colour of frames for you is based on your season and hair colour. When buying plastic frames, choose the same colour as your hair, but one shade lighter. If you are pale or sallow-skinned, do choose plastic frames, which bring colour to your face. Autumns in particular should consider this option.

Winters and *Summers,* the cool seasons, should make sure that their frames – particularly brown ones – are not reddish or golden. Even tortoiseshell must be a cool brown. If you choose metal frames, they should be silver-toned.

Autumns and *Springs,* the warm seasons, should choose plastic frames with a warm red or golden tone. Metal frames should be gold toned.

Colour Tints for Lenses

The best colour choices for tinted sunglasses, eye doctors say, are dark grey, green and brown. Choose the correct tint for your season – grey for the cool seasons, brown or green for the warm seasons. Avoid colours such as blue (which makes it difficult to distinguish the colour of traffic signals) lavender, orange, and rose (which screen out too little light to protect your eyes) and yellow (which actually intensifies the light).

For regular tinted glasses, choose no more than a 10 per cent tint. It is fashionable now, and attractive, to tint the top of the lenses in a neutral 30 per cent tint (say grey or brown, depending on your season), leave the centre plain, and tint the bottom in a 10 to 20 per cent tint. The effect is very subtle and flattering, but leaves your eyes free to see naturally out of the centre of your glasses.

Choosing the Right Shape

Glasses should complement the shape of your face. Choose frames that follow the shape of the top of your brow. The heaviness of the frames should be scaled to your bone structure.

You can adjust the width of the glasses frame for best effect. For most faces, keep the frames the same width as your temple. Choose them a *little* narrower to compensate for a wide face or a *little* wider for a narrower face. Too narrow and they'll look dinky, too wide and you'll look like a caricature!

Here are some tips for selecting frames to suit your face shape.

■ Oval
An oval face can wear any frame that is not extreme. Anything too large, too small or too angular will look unbalanced. Choose a style that suits your bone structure, clothing personality and season.

■ Round
A round face needs to create the illusion of cheekbones with frames that are straight across the top, angle inward toward the bottom and square off across the bottom. Avoid round glasses or curved sides, which will emphasise roundness. Severely square glasses are also wrong because the contrast in shapes is too extreme.

■ Square
Slightly rounded or curved frames with height on top can modify a too-square face. Since you want to lengthen the look of your face, aviator frames are handsome if your cheekbones are pronounced and gravity has not yet begun to make you jowly.

■ Rectangle
A rectangular face, being long and square, needs added width. A wide, square frame with slightly rounded corners or an overall rounded style is generally best.

Oval

Round

Square

Rectangle

Triangle

Since the triangular face has a broad forehead and narrow chin, you want glasses that create balance. The top piece of the frames should not be heavy, and the sides should not be wider than your temples. Consider glasses with a curved, dropped bottom piece. Square shapes are out, as is a heavy bridge.

ACCENTUATE THE POSITIVE

Once you have determined the general frame shape that is best for you, you can refine it even further to accentuate your best features and disguise your flaws.

If you have a long nose, choose glasses with a low bridge. A dark-coloured bridge is even more shortening.

If you have a short nose, a high, keyhole bridge in a light colour lengthens the appearance of your nose.

If your eyes are small or too close together, make them appear wider with a wide bridge. A clear bridge with coloured end pieces makes the illusion even stronger.

If your nose is wide or your eyes are wide set, choose a medium-weight dark-coloured bridge.

GOING, GOING, GONE: BALD CAN BE BEAUTIFUL, TOO

If you have thinning hair or are bald, don't despair. Yul Brynner and Telly Savalas have made baldness a symbol of virility, and Burt Reynolds, Sean Connery and others have shown that a hairpiece or transplant can be convincingly real. There are many options, and it is as important for you to know how to cut and take care of your hair as it is for a bushy-haired kid.

Keeping your hair *short* is the trick. Identify your facial shape and emphasise its assets. A good cut to create fullness is essential. Remember:

■ Keep thinning hair fairly short and always neatly trimmed. Long strands look sparse and *accentuate* baldness. Short, layered hair looks fuller than long hair.
■ Never part your hair over one ear and comb long strands over your bald spot. It only calls attention to your baldness and looks terrible when the wind blows. Really, bald *is* attractive if you will work with it instead of trying to cover it up.
■ If you have only a receding hairline, you *can* comb your hair forward. This does not look artificial, since some people wear their hair back to front anyway.
■ If you have just a few hairs on the top of your otherwise bald head, shave them off. It looks neater, smoother, and sexier and calls less attention to the top of your head.
■ Consider growing a moustache or a beard if your professional life permits. Facial hair can often balance baldness.

GROOMING

Please don't forget the details that ensure your attractiveness as a total person. Here's a grooming checklist.

■ Hair clean and neat.
■ Teeth brushed; good breath.
■ Deodorant – make sure it's still working.
■ Face shaved. (Watch for five o'clock shadow. Keep a razor at work.)
■ Fingernails clean and filed; cuticles trimmed.
■ Clothes clean, neatly pressed. (Check for hanging threads, loose buttons, sagging lining and split seams.)
■ Shirt cuffs and collars without frays.
■ Shoes polished, heels not worn.

You now have the tools to buy the best colours and clothing styles for you as well as a more organised approach to getting dressed.

Mix that with a great haircut, a neat and clean appearance, and you've got it all. Ready, set go, put your best look forward!

THE TOTAL MAN

Throughout this book we have stressed the outer you – your appearance, your image, your looks. But the true results of applying your colours are inner. The harmony and self-confidence that come with being comfortable with your appearance make you feel good. And your own special qualities are what make you valuable in your business life and that inspire affection in your personal life. Knowing that you look your best gives you the freedom and the confidence to continue to develop your full potential.

So here's to the Total Man! Enjoy your colours!

INDEX

*Major entries in the text are
indicated in bold type, illustrations
in italics.*

accessories 18, 20, 22, 24, 73,
  76, 77
analysis of colour 15-16
arms, proportion of 90, 96
Autumn man
  accessories 22
  basic colours 56, *59*, 61, 62
  basic wardrobe list 80
  business colours 22
  comparison with Spring 35
  comparison with Summer
    35
  co-ordinating wardrobe
    items 131, 133, 134
  examples of *28*
  eye colour 41, 42
  hair colour 41, 42
  leisure wear 23, 63
  prototypes 41
  shopping guide 22, 268-9
  skin colour 40, 41
  tie colours 122, 124

basic colours 16
basic wardrobe list **71-83**
body checklist 84, *86*

body, proportions of 84-94, *86*,
  116-17, *117*
bottom, size of 90, 96
business clothes, styles of 140,
  144, 147, *151*, 152, 155, 156,
  157, 158
business colours 49-50

casual wear, styles of 143, 146,
  149, 153, 155, 156, 157, 158
Classic clothing style 150-53,
  151, 158
Classic prototypes 153
clothing types and personality
  139-57
coat
  choice of 75, 77
  styles of 143, 146, 149-50,
    153
colour chart, guidelines for
  use **14-31**
colour comparison chart 66-8
co-ordination of wardrobe
  items **130-38**, *132*

deciding on season's colours
  33-47
Dramatic clothing style
  140-43, *141*, 155
Dramatic prototypes 143

eye colour 37, 38, 39, 40, 41,
  42, 43, 44

formal wear, styles of 143, 147,
  150, 153

glasses and face shape 176-9,
  177, 178
grooming **172-9**

hair, thinning 178
hairstyle and face shape
  172-5, *174*
height/weight proportion
  84-5, 90-91

image and colour 49
intensity of colour 14, 15

jacket, choice of 72, 75, 76, 77
jewellery, choice of 76, 143,
  146, 150, 153, 155, 156, 157,
  158

leg/body proportion *94*
leg/torso proportion 88, *88*, 93
leisure wear, styles of 19, *141*,
  142, 144, 146, 149, 152, 156,
  157, 158

mood and colour 49

neck, proportion of 90, 93, 96
Natural clothing style 147-50,
  148, 157
Natural prototypes 150

'old' clothes, choice of 75, 77

personality and colour 49

Romantic clothing style
  144-7, *145*, 156
Romantic prototypes 147

shirt 108-117
  basic 73
  casual 73
  choice of 74, 76, 77
  dressy 73
  fabric of 113-14
  fitting collar of 108-13, *109,
    111, 112, 115*, 115-16
  fitting cuff of 113, *113*, 116
  fitting shoulders of 116-17,
    117
  patterns of 114
  styles of 142, 146, 149, 155,
    156, 157
shoes
  choice of 74, 76, 77
  styles of 143, 146, 149, 153
shorts, choice of 74, 77
shopping guide 159-71
shoulder/hip proportion 85,
  91-2, *92*
shoulder slope 87, *87*, 92-3
slacks, choice of 76, 77
Spring man
  accessories 24
  basic colours *60*, 63-4, 81

basic wardrobe list 81
business colours 24, 64-5
comparison with Summer
  35
comparison with Winter 35
co-ordinating wardrobe
  items 131, 133, 134
examples of *29, 32*
eye colour 43, 44
hair colour 42-3, 44
leisure wear 25, 65
prototypes 43
shopping guide 24, 170-71
skin colour 42, 43
tie colour 122, 124
suit **97-107**
  choice of 72
  cut of 98-100, *99, 100*
  fabric of 107
  fitting jacket of 101-04, *102*
  fitting trousers of 104-06,
    105
  quality of 106-7
  size of 97-8
Summer man
  accessories 20
  basic colours 53-4, *58*
  basic wardrobe list 79
  business colours 20, 54-5
  comparison with Autumn
    35
  comparison with Winter 35
  co-ordinating wardrobe
    items 131, 133, 134
  examples of *27*
  eye colour 39, 40
  hair colour 39, 40
  leisure wear 21, 56
  prototypes 39

shopping guide 20, 166-7
skin colour 38, 39, 40
tie colours 122, 123
sweater, choice of 74, 77

tie **118-29**
  choice of 73, 76
  colour of 121-5
  length of *125*
  methods of tying 126-9, *127,
    128*
  patterns of 118-21, *119*
  styles of 142, 146, 149, 152,
    155, 156, 157, 158

uniforms 83

upper back, proportion of 90,
  96

waist/body proportion 89, *89,
  93, 95*
Winter man
  accessories 18
  basic colours 50-52, *57*
  basic wardrobe list 78
  business colours 18, 52-3
  comparison with Autumn
    35
comparison with Summer 35
co-ordinating wardrobe
  items 131, 133, 134
examples of *26, 32*
eye colour 37, 38
hair colour 37, 38
leisure wear 19, 53
prototypes 37, 38
shopping guide 18, 164-5
skin colour 37, 38
tie colours 121-2, 123

ACKNOWLEDGEMENTS

Photography John Waddy, Ben Rosenthal, Jacques Silberstein; *Illustrations* Yuki Horikawa; *Wardrobe and layout* Rob Hatherly, Pam Saunderson (Colour Me Beautiful Australia). *Photographs* page 99 Aquascutum, page 100 Cue at Austin Reed, page 145 Cue at Austin Reed, Page 148 Odermark, page 151 Austin Reed.

COLOUR FOR MEN

A division of Color Me Beautiful/ CMB Image Consultants

Personal Image Classes

CMB has a comprehensive network of highly trained image consultants who offer individual and group consultations for men and women on colour and style. As part of the consultation, CMB give each client an elegant wallet with 48 swatches representing their palette: the essential shopping guide.

CMB Products for Women

For the woman in your life, CMB offers exclusive ranges of cosmetics, scarves and fashion accessories available either from your local CMB image consultant, or by direct mail order.

A CMB Career

Image consulting is a growing industry. If you enjoy helping people make the most of themselves and are looking for a challenging and rewarding career, send for details and you will receive a free career pack on becoming a CMB image consultant. CMB operates a flexible career which can either be full-time from business premises or home, or can be run alongside an existing, compatible business.

CMB Seminars for Business Success

To help companies present their best image, CMB run corporate seminars in personal presentation and business etiquette.

For further details on the above services and products, please write to: **CMB Image Consultants**, FREEPOST, London SW8 3BR. Alternatively, call us direct on 071–627 5211.

CMB Image Consultants, 66 Abbey Business Centre, Ingate Place, London SW8 3NS